NEW PERSPECTIVES ON REGULATION

NEW PERSPECTIVES ON REGULATION

edited by David Moss *&* John Cisternino

THE
TOBIN PROJECT

Copyright © 2009 The Tobin Project, Inc.
All rights reserved. For information address
The Tobin Project, One Mifflin Place, Cambridge, MA 02138.

First Edition
10 9 8 7 6 5 4 3 2 1

Printed in the United States of America
This book is set in Adobe Caslon Pro.
Text design by Kristen Argenio/Ideal Design Co.

ISBN 978-0-9824788-0-6 (paperback)

Library of Congress Cataloging-in-Publication Data on file.

Visit www.tobinproject.org

Contents

New Perspectives on Regulation

New research in the social sciences has yielded insights with important (but, as yet, largely unrecognized) implications for the government's role in the economy. This new research holds the promise of enabling creative solutions to pressing problems. As the financial crisis unfolds and the global recession continues, the need to share these ideas beyond academia to inform policymaking and public debate has grown ever more urgent.

To this end, in the fall of 2008 the Tobin Project approached leading scholars in the social sciences with an unusual request: we asked them to think about the topic of economic regulation and share key insights from their fields in a manner that would be accessible to both policymakers and the public. Because we were concerned that a conventional literature survey might obscure as much as it revealed, we asked instead that the writers provide a broad sketch of the most promising research in their fields pertaining to regulation; that they identify guiding principles for policymakers wherever possible; that they animate these principles with concrete policy proposals; and, in general, that they keep academic language and footnotes to a minimum.

As if this weren't a tall enough order, we asked these scholars for one more thing: because the need for informed debate on our nation's problems is so great and the prospect of important new government action imminent, we asked that they prepare this new kind of essay on a compressed timeline measured in weeks rather than the many months or even years that traditional academic writing usually requires.

Fortunately, a group of leading scholars took up this challenge. This book is the product of their efforts, for which we are enormously grateful. In seven chapters, they condense lessons of a broad and varied swath of research and share insights for how we might address the financial crisis, ensure more enduring prosperity, and improve our regulatory institutions.

New Perspectives on Regulation is aimed primarily at citizens and public servants, including our leaders in Washington, who are grappling with a crisis that conventional approaches didn't predict and don't yet seem able to solve. But the breadth and accessibility of the work should also make it an excellent starting point for both students and scholars desiring a survey of the state of the art in the social sciences, particularly as it relates to public policy.

As an experiment in reconnecting academia to our broader democracy, *New Perspectives on Regulation* is one piece of the mission that the Tobin Project's affiliated scholars have undertaken: to invigorate public policy debate by rededicating their academic work to the pursuit of solutions to society's great problems.

Mitchell Weiss
Executive Director
The Tobin Project

Introduction

David Moss and John Cisternino

Regulation is suddenly back in fashion. After more than thirty years of deregulation being all the rage, the financial crisis of 2007 to 2009 has dramatically changed attitudes about the proper role of government. The market fundamentalism that drove far-reaching deregulation now looks more like a passing fad than the classic staple of political economy it was advertised to be.

At the same time, current thinking about regulation may not be as fresh as its promoters imagine, based to a large extent on ideas that were in vogue back in the 1960s. Market failure theory was then in its heyday. Every college student taking Econ 101 learned that although rational individuals typically maximized the welfare of the whole society simply by pursuing their own self-interest, Adam Smith's invisible hand occasionally (and sometimes spectacularly) broke down. A factory, for example, might spew too much smoke into the air if its owners did not have to bear the costs of the resulting pollution. Concern about "negative externalities" of this sort became a powerful justification and driver of environmental regulation. And this was just one piece of a larger whole, since market failure theory was used to justify a wide range of government interventions, from antitrust law to social insurance.

Market failure theory encompasses a powerful set of ideas, and it will inevitably remain a pillar of any modern approach to regulation. But it should not be the only—nor perhaps even the principal—intellectual foundation for a new era of regulatory engagement. Since the 1960s, influential new research on government failure has helped to drive the movement for deregulation and privatization. Yet even as the study of government failure was flourishing, some very different ideas were sprouting in the social sciences with profound implications for our understanding of human behavior and the role of government. Some of these ideas, particularly from the field of behavioral economics, have begun to nudge their way into discussions of regulatory purpose, design, and implementation. Yet even here, the process is far from complete; and many other exciting new lines of research—on everything from social cooperation to co-regulation—have hardly been incorporated at all.

Now that many lawmakers and their constituents have apparently concluded that the earlier focus on government failure went too far, it is imperative that they be able to draw on the very latest academic work in thinking anew about the role of government. This, at root, is the purpose of this book: to make the newest and most important research accessible to a broad audience, expanding our conception of both the possibilities and the potential pitfalls of economic regulation at a time of great turmoil in the global economy.

The seven chapters that follow offer seven different perspectives on the subject:

- **Market failure perspective.** Joseph Stiglitz gets things started in chapter 1 with a new look at market failure, which he suggests may be far more extensive—and more damaging—than generally believed.

- **Behavioral perspective.** In chapter 2, Eldar Shafir, Sendhil Mullainathan, and Michael Barr move beyond market failure, showing how a better understanding of the limits of individual rationality can inform better regulation—to protect consumers (against "teaser rates" in subprime mortgages, for example) and to ensure that markets reward producers who make us better off rather than exploit our limitations.

- **Cooperative perspective.** In chapter 3, Yochai Benkler suggests that self-interest is only a relatively small part of what drives human behavior, and he explores how successful experiments in social cooperation (in the collective production of Wikipedia, for example) can serve as a guide for the structuring and regulation of economic activity.

- **Risk management perspective.** Tom Baker and David Moss highlight the government's critical role as a risk manager in chapter 4; they reveal this as one of government's most important and successful functions (in policies ranging from Social Security to the FDIC) and, importantly, lay out the basic dos and don'ts of public risk management.

- **Experimental perspective.** Michael Greenstone argues in chapter 5 that we can dramatically strengthen regulation of all kinds by building experimentation into the process of policymaking, developing a culture of testing (modeled after medical drug and device testing) that privileges empirical evidence over theory in the making of regulatory policy.

- **Co-regulation perspective.** In chapter 6, Ed Balleisen and Marc Eisner take up the fascinating (and highly controversial) subject of co-regulation, drawing on a growing international literature to show how best to harness private industry in regulating itself and, at the same time, providing a clear set of criteria for when government-monitored self-regulation is most likely to succeed or fail.

- **International Perspective.** Finally, in chapter 7, Rawi Abdelal and John Ruggie adopt an international perspective, demonstrating the importance of seeing regulation as part of a larger societal bargain, in which citizens accept the risks and impositions of globalization in return for a degree of social security and a sense of shared values at home.

Although regulation is now back in fashion (at least for the time being), the success or failure of regulatory reform will ultimately be decided by substance rather than style. Policymakers must have access to the very best ideas; and they could soon find themselves on the defensive if they have to rely exclusively on the same ones that their predecessors depended on thirty or more years ago. Fortunately, in the intervening years, scholars have developed new ways of thinking about regulation—new perspectives that we hope will make a positive difference, helping to strengthen policymaking at this critical moment in the life of the nation.

CHAPTER I

Regulation and Failure

Joseph Stiglitz

Only under certain ideal circumstances may individuals, acting on their own, obtain "pareto efficient" outcomes, that is, situations in which no one can be made better off without making another worse off. These individuals involved must be rational and well informed, and must operate in competitive marketplaces that encompass a full range of insurance and credit markets. In the absence of these ideal circumstances, there exist government interventions that can potentially increase societal efficiency and/or equity.

Some of the major elements of these interventions are by now well accepted: antitrust laws, to prevent the creation of monopoly power and/or its abuse; consumer protection legislation, designed especially to address potential problems of exploitation arising from information asymmetries; and regulations to ensure the safety and soundness of the banking system, which are made necessary by systemic externalities (spillover effects of economic transactions affecting many people who were not parties to the transactions) that can arise when a "systemically" important institution fails, or is allowed to fail.

The current economic crisis has highlighted the need for government intervention in the event of the failure of a systemically important institution. But the need for massive intervention implies, in turn, the need to take actions to prevent the occurrence of such failures in the first place. Sometimes the damage done by actions that have adverse effects on others can be compensated for after the fact, but in the cases at hand, this is in general not possible. Policy interventions should be designed to make less likely the occurrence of actions that generate significant negative spillovers, or externalities.

But these are not the only reasons for government intervention. Markets fail to produce efficient outcomes for a variety of other reasons that economists have explored over the last twenty-five years. Markets are plagued by problems of information asymmetries, and there are incentives for market participants both to exploit and to increase these information asymmetries. For a variety of reasons key markets (such as those for insurance against some of the important risks that individuals and firms face) are missing. (Risk management is the principal subject of chapter 4 of this volume.)

Even when markets are efficient, they may fail to produce socially desirable outcomes. The wealthy and powerful may "exploit" others in an "efficient" way: the gains to one are offset by the losses to others, and in traditional economic parlance, so long as that is the case, markets are efficient. No one can be made better off without making someone else worse off. But such outcomes are socially unjust, and unacceptable. Governments impose regulations to prevent such exploitation and to pursue a number of other social goals.

These interventions take a variety of forms. Some are more intrusive than others. Some are more robust than others; that is, they can withstand attempts at circumvention. In recent decades, policy has focused on the design of packages of intervention that are robust, recognizing that the costs of the failure of intervention are typically on an order of magnitude greater than the costs of the interventions themselves. In financial markets, interventions include: (a) disclosure of information; (b) restrictions on incentive schemes (including conflicts of interest); (c) restrictions on ownership; (d) restrictions on particular behaviors; and (e) taxes designed to induce appropriate behaviors.

In addition, there are interventions to ensure competition. One of the big failures that the recent global financial crisis has exposed is that we allowed financial institutions to grow "too big to fail." Not only may such large institutions be able to exploit market power, but they also pose systemic risk to the economy and have perverse incentives that encourage such behavior. Institutions that grow too big to fail inevitably know that if they undertake high-risk activities and fail, government will pick up the pieces, but if they succeed, they walk away with the gains.

While regulation has typically focused on preventing "harmful" behaviors, there are some regulations that encourage "constructive" behaviors. These include CRA (Community Redevelopment Act) lending requirements, designed to ensure that there is a certain flow of credit to underserved communities.

Some interventions combine traditional equity concerns with market failures: governments may encourage private provision of retirement insurance (recognizing the social consequences of old-age poverty), but also recognize the abuses that may arise, unless there are restrictions to ensure that ordinary workers are treated symmetrically with management. Again, this crisis has exposed a regulatory failure: regulators failed to prevent the exploitation of poor and poorly educated borrowers by lenders. These people were not able to ascertain well the risks associated with various lending provisions, such as variable-rate mortgages with negative amortization, in a period in which interest rates were at a historically low level. The lenders should, of course, have been able to do a better job of risk assessment, but because of another set of market failures, they did not. The result is a massive social and economic disaster: people are losing their homes and their life savings, and our economy is facing a meltdown.

By its nature, a regulation restricts an individual or firm from doing what it otherwise would have done. Those whose behavior is so restricted may complain about, say, their loss of profits and potential adverse effects on innovation. But the purpose of government intervention is to address potential consequences that go beyond the parties directly involved, in situations in which private profit is not a good measure of social impact. Appropriate regulation may even advance welfare-enhancing innovations.

In short, regulation is necessary because social and private costs and benefits, and hence incentives, are misaligned. Such misalignment leads to problems not only in the short run but also in the long run. Incentives to innovate are distorted. America's financial system has been highly innovative, but to a great degree innovation has recently been directed at circumventing laws and regulations designed to ensure the efficiency, equity, and stability of the financial sector. Brokerages, banks, and insurance companies, among others, have been engaged, in effect, in accounting, tax, and regulatory arbitrage. But our financial system did not innovate in truly important ways that would have enabled Americans to better manage the risks they face—failing even to help manage the relatively simple risk of financing most people's most important asset, their home.

The design of regulatory structures and systems has to take into account: (a) asymmetries of information, since the regulator is often at an informational disadvantage relative to the regulated; (b) moral hazard, since there are often problems in ensuring that a regulator's behavior is consistent with social welfare (for example, that he/she is not beholden to those whom he/she is supposed to be regulating); and (c) human fallibility, since mistakes are inevitable, and we need to minimize the costs of such mistakes. Well-designed regulations take into account the limitations of implementation and enforcement. While no regulatory system is perfect, economies with well-designed regulations can perform far better than those with inadequate regulation. Regulations can both enhance markets and protect those who might otherwise suffer in unregulated markets.

Adam Smith and the Theory of Market Failures

No idea has had greater impact on policy than Adam Smith's notion that profit-maximizing firms interacting with rational consumers in competitive markets are led, as if by an "invisible hand," to society's general well-being. Smith was far more aware of the limitations of the market than his latter-day followers. Today, we realize that the reason that the invisible hand often seems invisible is that it is not there. Instead, we see a host of pervasive market failures, circumstances in which markets produce too much of some things (such as pollution) and too little of others (such as innovation). Whenever there are important imperfections and asymmetries of information (that is, situations in which one party knows something different from what others know), markets are not in general efficient. But such problems mean that markets are almost never fully efficient. The relatively recent recognition by economists of this phenomenon has had a profound effect in changing presumptions (Greenwald and Stiglitz 1986).[1] Previously the presumption that markets were efficient was widespread, with the corollary that only under exceptional circumstances (such as monopoly and massive pollution) were there failures that warranted intervention. Now, among mainstream economists, there is no presumption that markets are efficient. Government interventions thus necessarily need to focus on areas where market failures are most pronounced, such as in the health and finance sectors. In my remarks here, I focus on finance, because this area illustrates most of the key issues and is the subject of crucial current policy discussions.

The most obvious aspect of market failure in finance is associated with systemic externalities: as noted above, these are failures in the financial sector that have systemic effects. Those outside the financial sector today are suffering as a result of the mistakes made by those working in the sector. In making their decisions (for example, about lending practices), they did not take into account the systemic consequences of their actions. They never asked, If our loans go bad, what would happen to the entire economy? They looked only to their own balance sheets.

But looking deeper into the financial sector, we see a further set of problems: the incentives of those making the lending decisions were not aligned even with their shareholders' interests. The bonus system in place allowed them to reap large rewards when things went well while allowing them to evade the consequences when things went badly. These incentive structures encouraged shortsighted and excessively risky behavior. The banks' shareholders have not even been served well. This highlights another market failure: the separation of ownership and control, emphasized by Adolphe Berle and Gardiner Means, whose conclusions I have worked to set on more rigorous information-theoretic foundations (Stiglitz 1985). Such problems of corporate governance came to the fore in the aftermath of the Enron scandal, but the Sarbanes-Oxley Act of 2002 did not fully address the problem, since it left in place stock options, which not only provide asymmetric incentives but also provide incentives for bad accounting, allowing executives to increase their pay by providing information to shareholders that leads to higher share prices. Such market manipulation encourages the kind of off–balance-sheet behavior that played a major role in fomenting the current crisis.

Much of the proposed financial market regulatory reform focuses on precisely these problems: we need better corporate governance, to reduce the likelihood of these perverse incentives; and in the case of banks, where perverse incentives lead to drastic systemic consequences, with great costs to the economy and to taxpayers, we need direct restrictions on the form of compensation offered to executives. Compensation should be based on long-term performance, with far fewer asymmetries in the treatment of gains and losses. Stock options in particular need to be restricted. At the very least, shareholders should be aware of the consequences of offering stock options as part of executive pay packages in terms of share dilution. Banks that use stock options (or which otherwise maintain incentive structures encouraging excessively risky behavior) need to be subject to tighter supervision.

Because banks (or bank officials) do not always have any incentive for transparency—indeed, there may even be incentives for a lack of transparency (Edlin and Stiglitz 1995)—we need strong regulations concerning transparency and accounting, including regulation of the practice of marking assets to market. Without adequate regulations, it is possible to obtain only a very inaccurate picture of the liquidity and solvency of banks. Moreover, a lack of regulation also gives rise to perverse incentives that encourage banks to realize the gains in assets that have gone up in value and leave on their books those that have decreased in value. Worse still, knowing that they can thereby give a biased view of their position, banks then have an incentive to engage in excessive risk taking. The current crisis has exposed some of the problems that arise from inappropriate use of mark-to-market accounting by regulators, but that should not undermine efforts to enhance market transparency through mark-to-market accounting. What the system needs is a change in the use to which this information is put, and the elimination of incentives to obfuscate the information provided.

Managers often have an incentive to obfuscate, and standard transparency regulations by themselves may not go far enough. The problem with many derivatives was that they were so complex that even if all the information about them had been disclosed, most market participants would not have been able to assess their real value. Exchange-traded derivatives would have provided most of the risk management services needed, but in a more transparent way, with more competitive pricing. We will need to develop regulations restricting or inhibiting the use of over-the-counter derivatives, at least for banks and other systemically important institutions.

Because taxpayer money is at risk when a bank fails, excessively risky behavior needs to be directly circumscribed. Thus, we need much tighter restrictions on leverage. Ideally, these restrictions should be countercyclical, to discourage excessive lending in booms and to encourage more lending in recessions. (Such interventions illustrate another important class of "externalities," those associated with macroeconomic behavior.) Typically, the quality of bank lending goes down when banks expand lending rapidly, and this factor should be reflected in bank regulation and supervision.

Some have suggested that depositors should play a bigger role in bank supervision. Providing deposit insurance gives rise to "moral hazard," removing the incentive to supervise. But the current crisis should make clear how impossible it would be for any ordinary depositor to really monitor what is going on in a given bank. In this case, monitoring is a public good—something that everyone in society would benefit from—and should be provided publicly.

Market and Individual Irrationality

Much of modern economic theory has been predicated on the assumption of rational individuals and profit-maximizing firms interacting in competitive markets. Government policy has been directed at ensuring that markets are competitive—even Adam Smith recognized that there were strong incentives on the part of firms to engage in anticompetitive behavior. It is often easier to increase profits by restricting competition than by coming up with a better product.

By the same token, modern discussions of corporate governance have highlighted the ways in which modern corporations are often not well described by the standard "Marshallian" theory of profit- (or stock market value-) maximizing firms. The separation of ownership and control has meant that decisions are often made by managers, whose interests are not necessarily well aligned with other stakeholders, including shareholders. (Moreover, modern economic theory reveals that, given imperfect and asymmetric information and imperfect risk markets, even shareholder-value maximization—and especially shortsighted shareholder value maximization—may not be in society's interest (Stiglitz 2008).

I have discussed above the regulatory implications of both of these market imperfections. The assumption that individuals necessarily make rational economic decisions, however, has gone largely unassailed until recently. It is not, of course, that anyone really believes that individuals are always fully rational. But economic theorists have worried that without the assumption of full rationality, economists would be unable to say anything meaningful about individual behavior. But recent research has made it clear that individuals often act systematically in a way markedly different from that predicted by models of rationality. (Daniel Kahnemann received the Nobel Memorial Prize in economics in 2002 for his work, much of it in collaboration with the late Amos Tversky, in analyzing these irrationalities. This work has grown into a major subfield, called behavioral economics. For a fuller treatment of these issues, see chapter 2 of this volume.) The failure of people to act rationally is especially important in risk assessment—which is, of course, central to financial markets. An analysis of what went wrong in the financial markets to cause the current crisis shows a host of "irrationalities," behaviors that are hard to reconcile with any model of rational individuals and firms. Indeed, anyone looking at the history of bubbles, manias, and panics would find it hard to reconcile such behaviors with rationality (Kindleberger 2005). Alan Greenspan had called attention to these irrationalities in his famous "irrational exuberance" speech of December 1996, but in spite of an awareness of such irrationality, he continued to believe that market participants were sufficiently rational that they would not undertake undue risk. It was this belief that led to the widespread confidence that self-regulation would work. As Greenspan admitted in his recent Congressional testimony (Greenspan 2008) in the aftermath of the meltdown, the crisis shattered this belief. Self-regulation was based on a flawed confidence in rationality. (For new ideas on co-regulation, see chapter 6 of this volume.)

If this "flawed" rationality had affected only the parties directly involved in a given transaction, its effects would have been limited. But flawed rationality affected the entire economy. Thus, as Greenspan finally admitted, it is not enough to rely on rational behavior to ensure that individuals and firms undertake "prudent" risks.

But there was another flaw in Greenspan's analysis: even if each individual or firm were rational, that would not ensure systemic stability. There are externalities. This is critical to understanding the appropriate role of government in regulation. Earlier approaches focused on, for instance, protecting individual investors from abusive practices, or ensuring the safety and soundness of particular institutions. More recent discussions have focused on ensuring that "systemically significant institutions" are well regulated. However, what we have seen is a systemic failure, and such systemic failures can also arise from the correlated behavior of a large number of institutions, none of which is itself systemically significant. They can arise whether market participants are rational or not. But pervasive and persistent irrationalities—including flawed risk perceptions—may make such systemic failures more likely and provide a strong rationale for comprehensive government regulation of financial markets.

Regulatory Failure

So far, I have discussed a number of market failures within the financial sector that could be addressed by appropriate regulation. It is clear that our regulatory structure failed. Evidently, there was market failure, but there was also government failure. The primary reason for the government failure was the belief that markets do not fail, that unfettered markets would lead to efficient outcomes, and that government intervention would simply gum up the works. Regulators who did not believe in regulation were appointed, with the inevitable outcome that they did not do a very good job of regulating.

There is now a widespread consensus on the need for regulation, but that still leaves open the question: even if we have good regulations, how do we ensure that they will be enforced? How do we prevent regulatory failure?

There is no easy answer, but the approach that the Unites States has by and large taken is I think correct: multiple oversight, a broad system of checks and balances. The costs of duplication are far less than the costs of mistakes. The attorney general of New York has partially filled in for the deficiencies in the Securities and Exchange Commission. Tort law provides incentives for firms not to engage in egregious behavior.[2] There may have been abuses in class-action suits; but now, we may have excessively weakened this important part of our economy's incentive system.

Another part of the answer is to ensure that the voice of those whose interests are likely to be hurt by failure are well represented in the regulatory structures. Too often, the regulatory system gets captured by those that are supposed to be regulated. They are, after all, the "experts" who understand the system. The risk is especially severe in a political system such as ours, which is highly dependent on campaign contributions. But capture also occurs in a more subtle way: through the promulgation of ideas. When AT&T was threatened with a breakup under antitrust laws, its supporters objected that what mattered was not the actual level of competition in the telecommunications marketplace, but only *potential* competition. Similarly, the financial sector in recent years actively promoted the idea that markets could be self-regulating.

The current system has made regulatory capture too easy. The voices of those who have benefited from lax regulation are strong; the perspectives of the investment community have been well represented. Among those whose perspectives need to be better represented are the laborers whose jobs would be lost by macro-mismanagement, and the pension holders whose pension funds would be eviscerated by excessive risk taking.

One of the arguments for a financial products safety commission, which would assess the efficacy and risks of new products and ascertain appropriate usage, is that it would have a clear mandate, and be staffed by people whose only concern would be protecting the safety and efficacy of the products being sold. It would be focused on the interests of the ordinary consumer and investors, not the interests of the financial institutions selling the products.

Reducing the risk of regulatory capture must, of course, play an important role in the design of financial services regulations. Simple and transparent regulatory systems with limited regulatory discretion may be more immune to regulatory capture. There is a cost, for example, in the reduced scope for tailoring regulation to the circumstances at hand. But in many circumstances, that cost is far less than the benefit that arises from regulatory certainty.

Broader Social Objectives

So far, I have focused mostly on the single objective of ensuring the safety and soundness of the financial system (which entails more than just the safety and soundness of individual banks). But there are several other social and economic objectives of financial sector regulation.

As I noted in the introduction, one of the problems that has become manifest in this crisis is that financial institutions have grown too big to fail. Such large institutions not only represent a threat to competition—and without competition, markets are not efficient—but, again, they also create perverse incentives. As I noted in the opening of this essay, institutions that grow too big to fail have an incentive to undertake excessive risk, since their directors know that if the risks pay off, they get to keep the proceeds, but if they fail, taxpayers will pick up the pieces. Elsewhere, I have referred to this new form of "socialism" as "socialism American style"—privatizing gains but socializing losses. Regulators have a responsibility to ensure that institutions do not grow too big to fail (and in many cases, too big to be managed). There is little convincing evidence that there are substantial economies of scale sufficient to offset the adverse incentives to which such gigantism gives rise.

As we noted, an awareness of the risks of regulatory failure, including those resulting from regulatory capture, should play an important role in regulatory design. For instance, the costs of allowing financial institutions to grow too big are now apparent; the benefits of size—the economies of scale and scope—are questionable. But long experience should have taught us that financial institutions will try to use their political influence to weaken constraints on their size and reach, and in some cases they will succeed. If for one reason or another governments are unable to restrict the size of these institutions and prevent the development of too-big-to-fail institutions, regulators need to exercise intensive scrutiny, including restrictions on incentive structures that give rise to excessive risk taking and on the excessively risky practices themselves. To be sure, financial institutions will try to weaken such regulations, but by having a system with multiple checks—regulations of both products and institutions, at both the state and federal levels—we make regulatory circumvention and erosion of regulatory controls more difficult. There is a cost, as always, but it should be evident that the costs of insufficient oversight are far greater.

Financial markets also fail to make access to credit available to certain underserved groups. This may be because of discrimination. But, more generally, social returns to lending may not accord with private returns. Society may have an interest in ensuring inclusive growth and more broadly pursuing objectives of social justice, and there may be a variety of instruments with which it can and should do this (*see* for example chapter 7 of this volume, on "embedded liberalism.") The old "neoclassical" model (the same model in which Adam Smith's invisible hand worked) argued that distributional goals should be achieved solely through "lump sum" (that is, nondistortionary) tax redistributions. No government does this, and for good reason: the information that would be required to implement such a scheme makes it totally unrealistic. All redistributive schemes thus have, at the same time, allocative effects, and, in general, it is optimal to use a variety of instruments—including interventions such as the Community Reinvestment Act, which directs banks to allocate a certain fraction of the lending capacity to serve underserved communities.

Other Issues in Regulatory Design

There are many complex institutional issues that the market-failure approach to regulation raises, especially concerning the optimal form of government intervention, given the limitations of government, including government's often disadvantageous position relative to those that it is supposed to regulate (for example, public sector pay is lower than salaries in the private sector; there are information asymmetries, etc). In this short essay, I can only address a few of these.

First, the task of regulators is different from the task of those who create risky financial products, just as the skills (and pay) of those who test drugs are different from those who create them. The regulators' task is in some ways simpler: to ascertain safety and effectiveness. So too in financial-market regulation. The enforcement of simple regulatory restrictions (such as those on leverage and "speed bumps") requires different skills than the design of new regulations. To be sure, regulators have to be aware of the strong incentives for regulatory arbitrage and evasion and attempt to guard against these risks.

That is one of the reasons that much of regulation should focus on simple regulations, such as strict limits on leverage. Off–balance-sheet activities and tailor-made products should be looked at askance, if not simply forbidden, at least for commercial banks.

There is, here, an important tension between the concern, discussed earlier, in trying to prevent regulatory capture and the need to prevent innovative regulatory arbitrage. We argued earlier that concerns about regulatory capture suggest limited discretion. But innovative strategies of regulatory evasion require regulators to ascertain whether there is, for instance, "hidden leverage." New York's Martin Act (aimed at combating financial fraud) has been used effectively to curb certain "creative" abusive practices, but only because New York has had a series of attorneys generals who have been committed to using the law. They have focused on stopping the abusive practices rather than punishing the guilty parties.

The incentive for regulatory arbitrage also explains why regulation has to be comprehensive: if there is a highly regulated banking system, there will be incentives to move banklike activities into a shadow banking system, with equally disturbing systemic risks.

The strong incentives for regulatory evasion and arbitrage, combined with the inherently disadvantageous position of regulators, also explains why regulation has to focus both on products and institutions and on the overall economic/financial system. Awareness of the strong incentives for regulatory evasion and arbitrage, together with awareness of the asymmetries in costs and benefits (the costs of failures being borne by society, the benefits accruing to a few private parties), suggest that regulators should be both proactive and cautious. Complex products that seemingly serve no good risk-mitigation function should perhaps be banned, or at least restricted in usage, say to small hedge funds that are not highly leveraged. The costs of delay in introducing such products into the market would be relatively low—certainly much lower than the costs of the current crisis.

Some have focused on the fact that even with the best of regulators and regulations, there will be regulatory evasion. But this is not an argument against good regulations. To paraphrase the argument put forward by Paul Volcker in the midst of the East Asia crisis of 1997, even a leaky umbrella provides some protection in the midst of a thunderstorm. In arguing for restrictions on capital flows, I have used another analogy: a dam is not intended to stop the flow of water from the mountain to the sea, but even an imperfect dam may help protect people from a flood.

Concluding Comments

Markets are at the center of every successful economy. But unfettered markets often do not serve society well. Over the past two hundred years, economic theory and historical experience has shown that financial markets often fail to perform their essential functions of managing risk and allocating capital well, with disastrous social and economic consequences. While we have taken great pride in the success of our financial sector, a good financial sector would not only have performed these tasks better than ours has recently, but it also would have done so at much lower costs. Finance is a means to an end, not an end in itself. A good financial sector would have used few of society's resources; in a competitive financial sector, profits would have been low. Our financial sector was large, and it garnered a third of corporate profits. Some of the profits were based on exploitation of the poor; some were based on noncompetitive practices in credit card lending. It is hard to escape the conclusion that the sector did not serve our society well; and now, the costs that it has inflicted on the global economy are enormous. It is not just the trillions of dollars of taxpayer money that have been put at risk. The shortfall in production between the economy's potential and actual output will, cumulatively, also amount to trillions of dollars. Even a rich society can ill afford such waste.

That there is a need for better regulation now appears to be self-evident. But there will be those who will push for cosmetic reforms, not the deep reforms that are required.

In this paper, I have tried to outline the market-failure approach to reform, with especial application to the financial sector. This approach provides clear guidelines for the range and scope of requisite regulation and, together with the theory of government and regulatory failure, also provides guidelines for the design of a new regulatory system, one that will not only make such failures less likely in the future, but that will help ensure that the financial sector performs the vital role that it needs to perform in a dynamic modern economy.

Notes

1 Throughout this book, short-form citations are given in the run of text wherever possible. Full references may be found in the list of references at the end of each essay.

2 I am taking an expansive view of "regulation" in this paper. Regulation is any intervention in the market that changes behavior from what it otherwise would have been. Thus taxation should be viewed as part of the regulatory system, but so too should tort law. Tort law is directed at correcting one important set of externalities, those that arise when the actions of one individual "hurt" another. By forcing the individual who imposes the damage to compensate the injured party, tort law brings incentives better into alignment. It partially corrects the externality. But tort law has several limitations. First, it corrects the damage ex post, and in some cases, that may be too late. Indeed, it may be impossible to recover adequate compensation. Second, when many individuals are injured—that is, when the costs are diffuse—it is difficult for them to act together to secure appropriate compensation. Class-action suits are an imperfect attempt to address this problem. Finally, the legal system is very costly. In the current context, we can see these limitations very clearly. It would be difficult, if not impossible, for the millions of Americans—and those around the world—who have been injured by the actions of the financial system to receive adequate compensation for what they have suffered. The companies that have inflicted the damage are, in many cases, bankrupt. Each would claim that the global consequences are largely the result of the actions of others.

References

Edlin, Aaron, and Joseph E. Stiglitz. "Discouraging Rivals: Managerial Rent-Seeking and Economic Inefficiencies." *American Economic Review* 85 no. 5 (December 1995): 1301–12. Previously published as National Bureau of Economic Research Working Paper 4145, 1992. Available at http://www.nber.org/papers/w4145.

Greenspan, Alan. "The Challenge of Central Banking in a Democratic Society." Address delivered at Annual Dinner and Francis Boyer Lecture of the American Enterprise Institute for Public Policy Research, Washington, D.C. December 5, 1996. Available at http://www.federalreserve.gov/boarddocs/speeches/1996/19961205.htm.

———. Testimony at House Committee of Government Oversight and Reform hearing on the Financial Crisis and the Role of Federal Regulators, October 23, 2008. Available at http://oversight.house.gov/documents/20081023100438.pdf.

Greenwald, Bruce, and Joseph E. Stiglitz. "Externalities in Economies with Imperfect Information and Incomplete Markets." *Quarterly Journal of Economics* 101, no. 2 (May 1986): 229–64.

Kindleberger, Charles. *Manias, Panics, and Crashes: A History of Financial Crises.* 5th edition. Hoboken, NJ: John Wiley & Sons, 2005.

Stiglitz, Joseph E. "Credit Markets and the Control of Capital." *Journal of Money, Banking, and Credit* 17, no. 2 (May 1985): 133–52.

———. "Banks versus Markets as Mechanisms for Allocating and Coordinating Investment." In J. A. Roumasset and S. Barr, eds., *The Economics of Cooperation: East Asian Development and the Case for Pro-Market Intervention.* Boulder, CO: Westview Press, 1992. (Originally presented at Investment Coordination in the Pacific Century: Lessons from Theory and Practice Conference, University of Hawaii, January 1990.)

———. "Regulating Multinational Corporations: Towards Principles of Cross-Border Legal Frameworks in a Globalized World Balancing Rights with Responsibilities" (The Ninth Annual Grotius Lecture). *American University International Law Review* 23, no. 3 (2008): 451–558.

———. "Lessons for Economic Theory from the Global Financial Crisis" (Presidential Lecture to the Eastern Economic Association). *Eastern Economic Journal.* Forthcoming 2009.

CHAPTER 2

The Case for Behaviorally Informed Regulation

Michael S. Barr, Sendhil Mullainathan, Eldar Shafir

Policymakers approach human behavior largely through the perspective of the "rational agent" model, which relies on normative, a priori analyses of the making of rational decisions. This perspective is promoted in the social sciences and in professional schools, and has come to dominate much of the formulation and conduct of policy. An alternative view, developed mostly through empirical behavioral research, provides a substantially different perspective on individual behavior and its policy implications. Behavior, according to the empirical perspective, is the outcome of perceptions, impulses, and other processes that characterize the impressive machinery that we carry behind the eyes and between the ears. These proclivities, research has shown, intrude upon and shape behavior, often quite independently of deliberative intent, and in contrast with normative ideals that people endorse upon reflection. The results are systematic behaviors that are unforeseen and misunderstood by classical policy thinking. A more nuanced behavioral perspective, such research suggests, can yield deeper understanding and improved regulatory insight.

For example, while the causes of the recent mortgage crisis are myriad, a central problem was that many borrowers took out loans that they did not understand and could not afford. Their behavior is inconsistent with a model of rational agents with perfect information and perfect foresight, and good regulation ought to take their rather common behavior into account. As discussed below, an opt-out home mortgage plan, such as one that provides a standard fixed-rate loan with straightforward terms, could be a start. A person could then choose to opt out in favor of another mortgage plan, but only after being shown comprehensible disclosures about the risks involved. Lenders will have an incentive to make such disclosures properly because they will bear greater liability or other costs in the case of default among those who have opted out. In what follows, we outline the main tenets of the behavioral perspective, we provide some examples of relevant policy applications, and we discuss the implications of this analysis for the conduct of policy, particularly in the context of a market economy.

I. Human Behavior

In contrast with the rational agents of the classical theory, who make well informed, carefully considered, and fully controlled choices, behavioral research has shown that the availability of data does not always lead to effective communication and knowledge; understanding and intention do not necessarily lead to a desired action; and purportedly inconsequential contextual nuances can shape behavior and alter choices, often in ways that people themselves agree diminish their well-being in unintended ways.

I.1 Context

Human behavior turns out to be heavily context dependent, a function of both the person and the situation. One of the major lessons of modern psychological research is the impressive power that the situation exerts, along with a persistent tendency among people to underestimate that power relative to the presumed influence of intention, education, or personality traits. Various studies have documented the stunning capacity of situational factors to influence behaviors that are typically seen to reflect deep-seated personal predispositions. In his now-classic obedience studies, for example, Milgram (1974) showed how decidedly mild situational pressures sufficed to generate persistent willingness on the part of regular people to administer what they believed to be grave levels of electric shock to innocent subjects. Along similar lines, Darley and Batson (1973) recruited seminary students to deliver a practice sermon on the parable of the Good Samaritan. While half the seminarians were told they had plenty of time, others were led to believe they were running late. On their way to give the talk, all participants passed an ostensibly injured man slumped and groaning in a doorway. Whereas the majority of those with time to spare stopped to help, a mere 10 percent of those who were running late stopped, the remaining 90 percent stepping over the victim and rushing along. In contrast with these participants' ethical training and scholarship, the contextual nuance of a minor time constraint proved decisive in the decision not to stop and help a suffering man. As we analyze further below, the heavier-than-anticipated impact of context on behavior increases the importance and responsibility of effective regulation.

I.2 Decisional Conflict

On a less dramatic note, but of substantial policy relevance, are findings regarding the contextual impact of decisional conflict. People's preferences are typically constructed, not merely revealed, during the decision-making process (Lichtenstein and Slovic 2006), and the construction of preferences can be heavily influenced by the nature and the context of decision, which can have nontrivial regulatory implications, particularly as regards the proliferation of alternatives.

The classical view of decision making does not anticipate nor does it consider the implications of decisional conflict. Each option according to this view is assigned a subjective value, or "utility," and the person then proceeds to choose the option assigned the highest utility. A direct consequence of this account is that offering more alternatives is a good thing, since the more options there are, the more likely the consumer is to find one that proves attractive.

In contrast, since preferences tend to be constructed in the context of a decision, choices often prove difficult to make. People often search for a compelling rationale for choosing one option over another, and whereas sometimes a compelling reason can be articulated, at other times no easy rationale presents itself, rendering the conflict between options hard to resolve. Such conflict can lead people to postpone the decision or to select a "default" option, and can generate preference patterns that are fundamentally different from those predicted by accounts based on value maximization. In particular, the addition of options can complicate (and, thus, "worsen") the decision outcome while the normative assumption is that added options only make things better.

Decisional conflict, for example, has been shown to yield a greater tendency to search for alternatives when better options are available but the decision is difficult than when relatively inferior options are available and the decision is easy, even when expectations are otherwise the same (Tversky and Shafir 1992). More generally, as choices become difficult, consumers naturally tend to defer decisions, often indefinitely (Iyengar and Lepper 2000; Shafir, Simonson, and Tversky 1993; Tversky and Shafir 1992). In one study, expert physicians had to decide about medication for a patient with osteoarthritis. These physicians were more likely to decline prescribing a new medication when they had to choose between two new medications than when only one new medication was available (Redelmeier and Shafir 1995); the difficulty of choosing between the two medications presumably led some physicians to recommend not starting either one. A similar pattern was documented with shoppers in an upscale grocery store, where tasting booths offered the opportunity to taste six different jams in one condition, or any of twenty-four jams in the second. Of those who stopped to taste, 30 percent proceeded to purchase a jam from the six-jams selection, whereas only 3 percent purchased a jam from the twenty-four–jam selection (Iyengar and Lepper 2000).

Bertrand, Karlan, Mullainathan, Shafir, and Zinman (2008) conducted a field experiment with a local lender in South Africa to assess the relative importance of various subtle psychological manipulations in the decision to take up a loan offer. Clients were sent letters offering large short-term loans at randomly assigned interest rates. In addition, several psychological features on the offer letter were also independently randomized, one of which was the number of sample loans shown: the offer letters displayed either one example of a loan size and term, along with respective monthly repayments, or it displayed four such examples. In contrast with standard economic prediction and in line with conflict-based predictions, higher take-up was observed under the one-example description than under the multiple-example version. The magnitude of this effect was large: the simple (one-example) description of the offer had the same positive effect on take-up as dropping the monthly interest on these loans by more than two percentage points. In a related finding, Iyengar, Jiang, and Huberman (2004) show that employees' participation in 401(k) plans drops as the number of fund options proposed by their employer increases.

Adherence to the default or status quo has also been observed in naturally occurring "experiments." One concerning insurance decisions occurred when New Jersey and Pennsylvania both introduced the option of a limited right to sue, entitling automobile drivers to lower insurance rates. The two states differed in their default option: New Jersey motorists needed to acquire the full right to sue (transaction costs were minimal: a signature), whereas in Pennsylvania, the full right to sue was the default, which could then be forfeited in favor of the limited alternative. Whereas only about 20 percent of New Jersey drivers chose to acquire the full right to sue, approximately 75 percent of Pennsylvania drivers chose to retain it (Johnson *et al* 1993). A second naturally occurring "experiment" was recently observed in Europeans' decisions about being potential organ donors (Johnson and Goldstein 2003). In some European nations drivers are, by default, organ donors unless they elect not to be, whereas in other European nations they are, by default, not donors unless they choose to be. Observed rates of organ donors are almost 98 percent in the former nations and about 15 percent in the latter—a remarkable difference, given the low transaction costs and the significance of the decision.

These and other studies show that minor contextual changes can alter what consumers choose in ways that are unlikely to relate to their ultimate utility. It suggests that a proliferation of alternatives, which is where consumer markets are typically headed, needs to be addressed and handled with care, rather than be seen as an obvious advantage. It also suggests that the determination of a default outcome, for example, rather than being conceived as a mere formality that can be effortlessly circumvented, needs to be chosen thoughtfully, since it acquires a privileged status. In effect, when multiple options or the status quo are inappropriately handled (intentionally or not) this can decrease social welfare.

I.3 Mental Accounting

In their intuitive mental accounting schemes, people compartmentalize wealth and spending into distinct budget categories, such as savings, rent, and entertainment, and into separate mental accounts, such as current income, assets, and future income (Thaler 1985; 1992). Contrary to standard assumptions of fungibility, people exhibit different degrees of willingness to spend from their various accounts, which yields consumption patterns that are overly dependent on current income and sensitive to labels so that, for example, people save and borrow (often at a higher interest rate) at the same time (Ausubel 1991).

An understanding of such proclivities may help design instruments that bring about more desirable outcomes. For example, given that people are susceptible to faulty planning, distraction, and procrastination, studies have shown that saving works best as a default. Participation in 401(k) plans is significantly higher when employers offer automatic enrollment (Madrian and Shea 2001), and because participants tend to retain the default contribution rates, savings can be increased if they agree to increased default deductions following future raises (Benartzi and Thaler 2004).

I.4 Construal

A simple but fundamental tension between classical economic analyses and modern behavioral research is captured by the role of psychological "construal." Agents in classical economic analyses are presumed to choose among objective options in the world. People, however, do not typically contemplate objective circumstances; rather, stimuli are mentally construed, interpreted, represented, and then acted upon. Behavior is directed not toward actual states of the world, but toward our mental representation of those states, and mental representations do not bear a one-to-one relationship to the thing they represent, nor do they necessarily constitute faithful renditions of actual circumstances. As a result, many well-intentioned policy interventions can fail, or succeed, because of the way in which they are construed by the targeted group. For example, people who are rewarded for a behavior they find interesting and enjoyable can come to attribute their interest in the behavior to the reward and, consequently, come to view the behavior as less attractive (Lepper, Greene, and Nisbett 1973). In one classic study, for example, children who were offered a "good player award" to play with magic markers—which they had previously done with great relish in the absence of extrinsic rewards—subsequently showed little interest in the markers when these were introduced as an unawarded classroom activity (in contrast with children who had not received an award and showed no decrease in interest.) Similarly, decisions can be changed when preceded by a related act that leads to differential construal of one's preferences. Several "foot-in-the-door" and "lowball" techniques are based on the premise that initial compliance with a small request leads people to be then more likely to comply with a larger one. In this vein, Freedman and Fraser (1966) have shown that subjects are more likely to put up a large DRIVE CAREFULLY sign on their lawn if they have already complied with a request to put up a smaller one or to sign a petition regarding careful driving, even when the requests were made by different people. Similarly, Cialdini, Cacioppo, Bassett, and Miller's (1978) subjects were more likely to go pick up United Way posters if they had initially agreed to display them, as compared to a group that had not first considered the more modest request.

Other behavioral factors can influence the outcomes of decisions in ways that standard analysis is likely to miss; however, a full summary is beyond our present purview. To list just a few, people often are not very good at predicting their future tastes or at learning from past experience (Kahneman 1994), and their choices can be influenced by anticipated regret (Bell 1982), by costs already incurred (Arkes and Blumer 1985; Gourville and Soman 1998), by overly optimistic planning (Buehler, Griffin, and Ross 1994) and by the effects of temporal separation, where high discount rates for future as compared to present outcomes can yield dynamically inconsistent preferences (Loewenstein and Elster 1992; Loewenstein and Thaler 1992). Contrary to standard assumptions, the psychological carriers of value are gains and losses, rather than anticipated final states of wealth, and attitudes toward risk tend to shift from risk aversion in the face of gains to risk seeking for losses (Kahneman and Tversky 1979). Also, people are loss averse (the loss associated with giving up a good is substantially greater than the utility associated with obtaining it (Tversky and Kahneman 1991). This, in turn, leads to a general reluctance to depart from the status quo, because what needs to be renounced is valued more highly than the anticipated benefits (Knetsch 1989; Samuelson and Zeckhauser 1988).

1.5 Knowledge and Attention

Standard theory assumes that consumers are attentive and knowledgeable, and typically able to avail themselves of important information. In contrast, there appears to be a rampant ignorance of options, program rules, benefits, and opportunities, and not only among the poor or the uneducated. Surveys show that fewer than one-fifth of investors (in stocks, bonds, funds, or other securities) can be considered "financially literate" (Alexander, Jones, and Nigro 1998), and similar findings describe the understanding shown by participants in pension plans—meaning, mostly, 401(k)s (Schultz 1995). Indeed, even older beneficiaries often do not know what kind of pension they are set to receive, or what mix of stocks and bonds they are invested in.

The amount of information people attend to is limited, and cognitive load has been shown to affect performance in everyday tasks. To the extent that consumers find themselves in challenging situations that are unfamiliar, distracting, or tense, all of which consume cognitive resources, fewer resources will be available to process the information that is relevant to the decision at hand. This, in turn, can make decision making even more dependent on situational cues and immaterial considerations. Furthermore, this is likely to be even more true for "low literate" participants, whose even more limited knowledge and understanding can lead them to experience difficulties with effort-versus-accuracy tradeoffs, to rely excessively on peripheral cues in product advertising and packaging, and even to withdraw systematically from market interactions (Adkins and Ozanne 2005, and references therein.) In summary, for participants with limited cognitive resources, whose decisions are heavily dependent on perceived norms, automatic defaults, and other minor contextual nuances, regulation merits even greater attention.

1.6 Context and Institutions

The substantial influence of context on behavior naturally implies that institutions will come to play a central role in shaping how people think and what they do. Among other things:

Institutions Shape Defaults

Institutions normally define defaults. Moreover, it is well established that defaults can have a profound influence on the outcomes of individual choices. Data available on decisions ranging from retirement savings and portfolio choices to the decision to be a willing organ donor illustrate the substantial increase in market share of default options (Johnson and Goldstein 2003; Johnson *et al* 1993). Although the default in an abstract sense appears to be merely one among a number of alternatives, in reality defaults benefit not only from confusion, procrastination, forgetting, and other sources of inaction, but they may also be perceived as the most popular option (this often becomes a self-fulfilling prophesy), or the option implicitly recommended.

Institutions Shape Behavior

Many low-income families are, in fact, savers, whether or not they resort to banks (Berry 2004). Without the help of a financial institution, however, their savings are at risk (including theft, impulse spending, and the needs of house-hold members), savings will grow more slowly, and may not be readily available to support access to reasonably priced credit in times of need. Institutions provide safety and control. In circumstances of momentary need, temptation, distraction, or limited self-control, those savers who are unbanked are likely to find it all the more difficult to succeed on the path to long-term prosperity. A recent survey conducted by the American Payroll Association shows that "American employees are gaining confidence in direct deposit as a reliable method of payment that gives them greater control over their finances, and that employers are recognizing direct deposit as a low-cost employee benefit that can also save payroll processing time and money."[1] The employers of the poor, in contrast, often neither require nor propose electronic salary payments. Instead, they prefer not to offer direct deposit to hourly, nonexempt employees, tem-porary or seasonal employees, part-timers, union employees, and employees in remote locations—all categories that correlate with being low paid. The most frequently stated reasons for not offering direct deposit to these employees include lack of processing time to meet standard industry ("Automatic Clearing House") requirements, high turnover, and union contract restrictions. All this creates a missed opportunity to offer favorable defaults to needy individuals, whose de facto default consists of going after hours to cash their check for a hefty fee.

Institutions Provide Implicit Planning

As it turns out, a variety of institutions provide implicit planning, often in ways that address potential behavioral weaknesses. Credit card companies send cus-tomers timely reminders of due payments, and clients can elect to have their utility bills automatically charged, allowing them to avoid late fees if occasion-ally they do not get around to paying in time. The low-income buyer, on the other hand, without the credit card, the automatic billing, or the Web-based reminders, risks missed payments, late fees, disconnected utilities (followed by high reconnection charges), etc. Interestingly, context can also be detrimental by providing debt too easily. Temporal discounting in general and present bias in particular can be exploited to make cash now more attractive than future costs appear menacing.

A behavioral analysis yields new appreciation for the impact and responsi-bility of financial institutions, which should be considered not merely from a financial cost-saving point of view, but, instead, should be understood to affect people's lives, by easing their planning, facilitating their intended actions, or enabling their resistance to temptation.

II. Interaction with Markets

The perspective outlined above, and the regulation it triggers, need to be embedded in the logic of markets. A framework is required that takes into account firm incentives and responses to behaviorally motivated regulation. This perspective produces two dimensions to consider. First, the psychological biases of individuals can either help or hurt the firms they interact with; hence firms' and public-minded regulators' interests are sometimes misaligned and sometimes not. Consider a consumer who does not understand the profound effects of the compounding of interest. Such a bias would lead the individual both to undersave, and to overborrow. Society would prefer that the individual did not have such a bias in both contexts. Firms, however, would prefer that the individual not have the bias to undersave, so that funds intended for investment and fee generation would not diminish (abstracting from fee structures), but, at least over the short term, firms would be perfectly content to see the same individual overborrow (abstracting from collection costs). Because people are fallible and easily misled, transparency does not always pay off and firms sometimes have strong incentives to *exacerbate* psychological biases by hiding borrowing costs. Regulation in this case faces a much more difficult challenge than in the savings situation. The market response to individual failure can profoundly affect regulation. In attempting to boost participation in 401(k) retirement plans, the regulator faces at worst indifferent and at best positively inclined employers seeking to boost employee retention and to comply with federal pension rules.[2] In forcing disclosure of hidden prices of credit, by contrast, the regulator often faces noncooperative firms, whose interests are to find ways to work around or undo interventions.

A second implication of our equilibrium model of firms in particular markets interacting with individuals with specific psychologies is that the mode of regulation chosen should take account of this interaction. We might think of the regulator as holding two different levers, which we describe as changing the rules and changing the scoring.[3] When forcing disclosure of the APR, for example, the regulator effectively changes the "rules" of the game: what a firm must say. A stronger form of rule change is product regulation: changing what a firm must do. Behavioral rule changes, such as creating a favored starting position or default, falls between these two types. When changing liability or providing tax incentives, by contrast, the regulator changes the way the game is "scored." Typically, changing the rules of the game (without changing the scoring, as through liability changes) maintains the firms' original incentives to help or hurt consumer bias, channeling the incentive into different behaviors by firms or individuals, while changing the scoring of the game can alter those incentives.

This perspective highlights the care that must be taken when transferring, for example, the insights of defaults in 401(k) participation to other domains. According to the present analysis, changing the rules on retirement saving (by introducing defaults) works well because employers' incentives align (or do not misalign) with regulatory efforts to guide individual choice. In other words, under current conditions, employers are either unaffected or may even be hurt by individuals' propensity to undersave in 401(k) plans.[4] They thus will not oppose an attempt to fix that problem. In other applications, where firms' incentives misalign with regulatory intent, changing the rules alone may not work well since firms may have the ability to work creatively around those rule changes. Interestingly, such circumstances may lead to regulations ("changing the scoring") which, though deeply motivated by behavioral insights, are not themselves particularly psychological in nature. That is, given market responses, psychological rules such as defaults or framing may be too weak, and changes in liability rules or other measures may be necessary, as we explain below.

This distinction in market responses to individual psychology is central to our framework and is illustrated in table 1. In some cases, the market is either neutral or wants to overcome consumer fallibility. In other cases, the market would like to exploit or exaggerate consumer fallibility. Thus, when consumers misunderstand compounding of interest in the context of *saving*, banks have incentives to reduce this misunderstanding so that they can increase their deposits. When consumers misunderstand compounding in the context of *borrowing*, lenders have little incentive to remove this misunderstanding, as it can only

Table 1. The Firm and the Individual

Behavioral Fallibility	Market neutral and/or wants to overcome consumer fallibility	Market exploits consumer fallibility
Consumers misunderstand compounding	Consumers misunderstand compounding in *savings* • Banks would like to *reduce* this to increase savings base	Consumers misunderstand compounding in *borrowing* • Banks would like to *exploit* this to increase borrowing
Consumers procrastinate	Consumers procrastinate in signing up for EITC • Tax filing companies would like to *reduce* this so as to increase number of customers	Consumers procrastinate in returning rebates • Retailers would like to *exploit* this to increase revenues

decrease the debts they are able to issue.[5] When consumers procrastinate in signing up for the EITC (and hence in filing for taxes) private tax preparation firms have incentives to discourage such procrastination so as to increase their customer base. When consumers procrastinate in returning rebates (but make retail purchases as if they are going to get a rebate), retailers benefit. Note the parallelism in these examples: firm incentives to alleviate or exploit a bias are not an intrinsic feature of the bias itself. Instead, they are a function of how the bias plays itself out in the particular market structure.

In the consumer credit market, we worry that many interactions between individuals and firms are of the kind in which firms seek to exploit rather than alleviate bias. If true, this raises the concern of overextrapolating from the 401(k) defaults example to credit products. To the extent that 401(k) defaults work because optimal behavior is largely aligned with market incentives, other areas, such as credit markets, might be more difficult to regulate with mere defaults. Furthermore, if the credit market is dominated by "low-road" firms offering opaque products that "prey" on human weakness, it is more likely that regulators of such a market will be captured because "high-road" interests are too weak to push back against low-road players; that market forces will defeat positive defaults sets; and that low-road players will continue to dominate. Many observers, for example, believe that the credit card markets are, in fact, currently dominated by such low-road firms (*see*, for example, Mann 2007; Bar-Gill 2004) and that formerly high-road players have come to adopt the sharp practices of their low-road competitors. If government policymakers want to attempt to use defaults in such contexts, they might need to deploy "stickier" defaults or more aggressive policy options.

In our approach to the issue of regulatory choice the regulator can either change the rules of the game or change the scoring of the game. Setting a default is an example of changing the rules of the game, as is disclosure regulation. Specifically, the rules of the game are changed when there is an attempt to change the nature of the interactions between individuals and firms, as when the regulation attempts to affect what can be said, offered, or done. Changing the scoring of the game, by contrast, changes the payoffs a firm will receive for particular outcomes. This may be done without a particular rule about how the outcome is to be achieved. For example, pension regulation that penalizes firms whose 401(k) plan enrollment is top-heavy with highly paid executives is an example of how scoring gives firms *incentives* to enroll low-income individuals without setting particular rules on how this is done. Changing rules and changing scoring often accompany each other, but they are conceptually distinct.

The discussion below illustrates how policies in the top right corner of table 2 face a particular challenge. Changing the rules of the game alone will be difficult when firms are highly motivated to find workarounds. As such, when we suggest opt-out policies in mortgages below, the challenge will be to find ways to make these starting positions "sticky" so that firms do not simply undo their default nature. In our judgment, both achieving a good default and figuring out how to make it work requires separating low-road from high-road firms and making it profitable for high-road firms to offer the default product (for a related concept, *see* Kennedy 2005). For that to work, the default must be sufficiently attractive to consumers, sufficiently profitable for high-road firms to succeed in offering it, and penalties associated with deviations from the default must be sufficiently costly so as to make the default "stick" even in the face of market pressures from low-road firms. It may be that in some credit markets, low-road firms have become so dominant that sticky defaults will be ineffectual. Moreover, achieving such a default is likely more costly than making defaults work when market incentives align, not least because the costs associated with the stickiness of the default involve greater deadweight losses given that there will be higher costs to opt out for those for whom deviating from the default is optimal. These losses would need to be weighed against the losses from the current system, as well as against losses from alternative approaches, such as disclosure or product regulation. Nonetheless, given the considerations above, it seems worth exploring whether such sticky defaults can help to transform consumer financial markets.

Table 2. Behaviorally Informed Regulation

	Market neutral and/or wants to overcome consumer fallibility	Market exploits consumer fallibility
Rules	Public education on saving Direct deposit/auto-save Licensing	Sticky defaults (opt-out mortgage or credit card) Information de-biasing on debt (full information disclosure, payoff time for credit cards)
Scoring	Tax incentives for savings vehicles IRS Direct Deposit Accounts	Ex post liability standard for truth in lending Broker fiduciary duty and/or changing compensation (Yield Spread Premiums)

The lessons of a more nuanced behavioral perspective are twofold. On the one hand, people's behavior is idiosyncratic, context dependent, and nuanced in ways that render simple normative assumptions misleading and, in general, complicate policy design. On the other hand, because behavior follows its own rules, policymakers have an added responsibility to concern themselves with appropriate context and detail, and a reason to hope that attention will lead to improved outcomes.

As noted above, because of likely market responses to psychological factors in different contexts, regulation may need to take a variety of forms, including some that while informed by psychology are not designed to affect behavioral change, but rather to alter the structure of the market in which relevant choices are made. In what follows, we consider behaviorally informed regulation in the context of mortgage, credit card, and banking markets, with specific proposals that fall into each bin. Given the complexities involved, our purpose is not to champion the specific policies below. Rather, we illustrate how a behaviorally informed regulatory analysis may lead to a deeper understanding of the costs and benefits, and to potentially improved designs, of specific policies.

III. Behaviorally Informed Policies

III.1 Behaviorally Informed Home Mortgage Regulation

Full Information Disclosure to De-bias Borrowers

With the advent of nationwide credit reporting systems and the refinement of credit scoring and modeling, creditors and brokers themselves, including not just their credit scores, but their likely performance regarding a particular set of loan products. Creditors will know whether borrowers could qualify for better, cheaper loans, as well as how likely it is that borrowers will meet their obligations under an existing mortgage, or become delinquent, refinance, default, or go into foreclosure. Yet lenders are not required to reveal this information to borrowers. At the same time, the lack of disclosure of such information is likely exacerbated by consumer beliefs. Consumers likely have false background assumptions regarding what brokers and creditors reveal to them about their borrowing status. What if consumers believe the following?

> Creditors reveal all information about me and the loan products I am qualified to receive. Brokers work for me in finding me the best loan for my purposes, and lenders offer me the best loans for which I qualify. I must be qualified for the loan I have been offered, or the lender would not have validated the choice by offering me the loan. Because I am qualified for the loan that must mean that the lender thinks that I can repay the loan. Why else would they lend me the money? Moreover,

the government tightly regulates home mortgages; they make the lender give me all these legal forms. Surely the government must regulate all aspects of this transaction.

In reality, the government does not regulate as borrowers believe, and lenders do not necessarily behave as borrowers hope. Instead, information is hidden from borrowers, information that would improve market competition and outcomes. Given consumers' probably false background assumptions and the reality of asymmetric information favoring lenders and brokers, we suggest that creditors be required to reveal useful information to borrowers at the time of a mortgage loan offer, including disclosure of borrowers' credit scores, and borrowers' qualifications for all of lenders' mortgage products. Brokers could even be required to reveal the wholesale rate sheet pricing—the rates at which lenders would be willing to lend to each type of borrower. Such an approach corresponds to the use of de-biasing information, in the top right of table 2.

The goal of these disclosures would be to put pressure on creditors and brokers to be honest in their dealings with applicants. The additional information might improve comparison shopping and perhaps outcomes. Of course, revealing such information would also reduce broker and creditor profit margins. But if the classic market competition story relies on full information, and assumes rational behavior based on understanding, we can view this proposal as simply attempting to remove market frictions from information failures, and move the market competition model more toward its ideal. By reducing information asymmetry, full information disclosure would help to de-bias consumers and lead to better competitive outcomes.

Ex Post Standards-based Truth in Lending

Optimal disclosure will not simply occur in all markets through competition alone. Competition under a range of plausible scenarios will not necessarily generate psychologically informative and actionable disclosure, as the current crisis in the subprime mortgage sector suggests may have occurred. If competition does not produce informative disclosure, disclosure regulation might be necessary. But simply because disclosure regulation is needed does not mean it will work. Regulating disclosure appropriately is difficult and requires substantial sophistication by regulators, including psychological insight.

A behavioral perspective could focus on improving disclosures themselves. The goal of disclosure should be to improve the quality of information about contract terms in meaningful ways. That would suggest, for example, that simply adding information is unlikely to work. Disclosure policies are effective to the extent that they present a frame—a way of perceiving the disclosure—that is both well understood and conveys salient information that helps the decision maker act optimally. It is possible, for example, that information about the failure frequency of particular products might help (for example, *Two out of ten borrowers who take this kind of loan default*), but proper framing can be difficult to achieve and to maintain consistently, given that it may vary across situations. Moreover, the attempt to improve decision quality through an improvement in consumers' understanding, which is presumed to change consumers' intentions to act, and finally their actual actions, is fraught with difficulty. There is often a gap between understanding and intention, and particularly between intention and action.

Furthermore, even if meaningful disclosure rules can be created, sellers can undermine whatever before-the-fact or ex ante disclosure rule is established, in some contexts simply by "complying" with it: *Here's the disclosure form I'm supposed to give you, just sign here.* For example, with rules-based ex ante disclosure requirements for credit, such as the Truth in Lending Act of 1968 (TILA), the rule is set up first, and the firm (the discloser) moves last. While an ex ante rule provides certainty to creditors, whatever gave the discloser incentives to confuse consumers remains in the face of the regulation. While disclosers may officially comply with a given rule, they will nonetheless remain susceptible to market pressure to find other means to avoid the salutary effects on consumer decisions that the disclosure is intended to achieve.

In light of the difficulties of addressing such issues ex ante, we propose that policymakers consider shifting away from sole reliance on a rules-based, ex ante regulatory structure for disclosure embodied in TILA and toward integration of an ex post, standards-based disclosure requirement as well. Rather than a rule, we would deploy a standard, and rather than an ex ante decision about content, we would permit the standard to be enforced after loans are made. In essence, courts or expert agencies would determine whether the disclosure would, under common understanding, have effectively communicated the key terms of the mortgage to the typical borrower. This approach could be similar to ex post determinations of reasonableness of disclaimers of warranties in sales contracts under UCC 2-316 (*see* White and Summers 1995). This type of policy intervention would correspond to a change in "scoring," in the lower right of table 2.

In our judgment, an ex post version of truth in lending based on a reasonable-person standard to complement the fixed disclosure rule under TILA might permit innovation—both in products themselves and in strategies of disclosure—while minimizing rule evasion. An ex post standard with sufficient teeth could change the incentives of firms to confuse and would be more difficult to evade. Under the current approach, creditors can easily "evade" TILA, by simultaneously complying with its actual terms and making the required disclosures regarding the terms effectively useless in the context of the borrowing decisions of consumers with limited attention and understanding. TILA, for example, does not block a creditor from introducing a more salient term (*Lower monthly cost!*) to compete with the APR for borrowers' attention. Under an ex post standards approach, by contrast, lenders could not plead compliance with TILA as a defense. Rather, the question would be one of objective reasonableness: whether the lender meaningfully conveyed the information required for a typical consumer to make a reasonable judgment about the loan. Standards would also lower the cost of specification ex ante. Clarity of contract is hard to specify ex ante but easier to verify ex post. Over time, through agency action, guidance, model disclosures, "no action" letters, and court decisions, the parameters of the reasonableness standard would become known and predictable.

While TILA has significant shortcomings, we do not propose abandoning it. Rather, TILA would remain (with whatever useful modifications to it might be gleaned from our increased understanding of consumers' emotions, thought processes, and behaviors). Quite recently, for example, the Federal Reserve Board unveiled major and useful changes to its disclosure rules, based in part on consumer research.[6] TILA would still be important in permitting comparison-shopping among mortgage products, one of its two central goals. However, some of the burden of TILA's second goal, to induce firms to reveal information that would promote better consumer understanding, would be shifted to the ex post standard.

Of course, there would be significant costs to such an approach, especially at first. Litigation or regulatory enforcement would impose direct costs and the uncertainty surrounding enforcement of the standard ex post might deter innovation in the development of mortgage products. The additional costs of compliance with a disclosure standard might reduce lenders' willingness to develop new mortgage products designed to reach lower-income or minority borrowers who might not be served by the firms' plain-vanilla products. The lack of clear rules might also increase consumer confusion regarding how to compare innovative mortgage products to each other, even while it increases consumer understanding of the particular mortgage products being offered. Even if we couple the advantages of TILA for mortgage comparisons with the advantages of an ex post standard for disclosure in promoting clarity, the net result may simply be greater confusion with respect to cross-loan comparisons. That is, if consumer confusion results mostly from firm obfuscation, then our proposal will likely help a good deal. By contrast, if consumer confusion in this context results mostly from market complexity in product innovation, then the proposal is unlikely to make a major difference, and other approaches focused on loan comparisons might be warranted (*see*, for example, Thaler and Sunstein 2008).

Despite the shortcomings of an ex post standard for truth in lending, we believe that such an approach is worth pursuing. To limit the costs associated with our approach, the ex post determination of reasonableness could be significantly confined. For example, if courts are to be involved in enforcement, the ex post standard for reasonableness of disclosure might be limited to providing a (partial) defense to payment in foreclosure or bankruptcy, rather than being open to broader enforcement through affirmative suit. Alternatively, rather than court enforcement, the ex post standard might be enforced by the bank regulators or another expert consumer agency,[7] through supervision and enforcement actions. The ex post exposure might be significantly reduced through ex ante steps. For example, regulators might develop safe harbors for reasonable disclosures, issue model disclosures, use "no action" letters to provide certainty to lenders, and the like. Moreover, firms might be tasked with conducting regular surveys of borrowers or conducting experimental design research to validate their disclosures, with positive results from the research providing rebuttable presumptions of reasonableness, or even safe harbors from challenge. The key is to give the standard sufficient teeth without deterring innovation. The precise contours of enforcement and liability are not essential to the concept, and weighing the costs and benefits of such penalties is beyond the scope of what we hope to do in introducing the idea here. Further work will be required to detail the design for implementation.

"Sticky" Opt-Out Mortgage Regulation

While the causes of the mortgage crisis are myriad, a central problem was that many borrowers took out loans that they did not understand and could not afford. Brokers and lenders offered loans that looked much less expensive than they really were, because of low initial monthly payments and costly hidden features. Families commonly make mistakes in taking out home mortgages because they are misled by broker sales tactics, misunderstand the complicated terms and financial tradeoffs in mortgages, wrongly forecast their own behavior and misperceive their risks of borrowing. How many homeowners really understand how the teaser rate, introductory rate, and reset rate relate to the London interbank offered rate plus some specified margin, or can judge whether the prepayment penalty will offset the gains from the teaser rate?

Improved disclosures might help. Altering the rules of the game of disclosure, and altering the "scoring" for seeking to evade proper disclosure, may be sufficient to reduce the worst outcomes. However, if market pressures and consumer confusion are sufficiently strong, such disclosure may not be enough. If market complexity is sufficiently disruptive to consumer choice, product regulation might prove most appropriate. For example, by barring prepayment penalties, we could reduce lock-in to bad mortgages; by barring short-term ARMs and balloon payments, we could reduce refinance pressure; in both cases, more of the cost of the loan would be pushed into interest rates and competition could focus on a consistently stated price in the form of the APR. Price competition would benefit consumers, who would be more likely to understand the terms on which lenders were competing. Product regulation would also reduce cognitive and emotional pressures related to potentially bad decision making by reducing the number of choices and eliminating loan features that put pressure on borrowers to refinance on bad terms. However, product regulation may stifle beneficial innovation and there is always the possibility that government may simply get it wrong.

For that reason, we propose a new form of regulation. We propose that a default be established with increased liability exposure for deviations that harm consumers. For lack of a better term, we call this a sticky opt-out mortgage system. As with opt-out regulation generally, a sticky opt-out system would fall, in terms of stringency, somewhere between product regulation and disclosure; however, for reasons we explain below, market forces would likely swamp a pure opt-out regime—that's where the need for stickiness comes in. This approach corresponds to a combination of changing the rules of the game, in the top right of table 2, and changing liability rules, at the bottom right of that table.

The proposal is grounded in our equilibrium model of firm incentives and individual psychology. Borrowers may be unable to distinguish among complex loan products and act optimally based on such an understanding (*see*, for example, Ausubel 1991). We thus deploy an opt-out strategy to make it easier for borrowers to choose a standard product, and harder for borrowers to choose a product that they are less likely to understand. At the same time, lenders may seek to extract surplus from borrowers because of asymmetric information about future income or default probabilities (*see* Musto 2007), and, in the short term, lenders and brokers may benefit from selling borrowers loans they cannot afford. Thus, a pure default would be undermined by firms, and regulation needs to take account of this market pressure by pushing back.

In our model, lenders would be required to offer eligible borrowers a standard mortgage (or set of mortgages), such as a fixed-rate, self-amortizing thirty-year mortgage loan, according to reasonable underwriting standards. The precise contours of the standard set of mortgages would be set by regulation. Lenders would be free to charge whatever interest rate they wanted on the loan, and, subject to the constraints outlined below, could offer whatever other loan products they wanted outside of the standard package. Borrowers, however, would get the standard mortgage offered, unless they chose to opt out in favor of a nonstandard option offered by the lender, after honest and comprehensible disclosures from brokers or lenders about the terms and risks of the alternative mortgages. An opt-out mortgage system would mean that borrowers would be more likely to get straightforward loans they could understand.

But for the reasons cited above, a plain-vanilla opt-out policy is likely to be inadequate. Unlike the savings context, where market incentives align well with policies to overcome behavioral biases, in the context of credit markets, firms often have an incentive to hide the true costs of borrowing. Given the strong market pressures to deviate from the default offer, we would need to require more than a simple opt-out to make the default sticky enough to make a difference in outcomes. Deviation from the offer would require heightened disclosures and additional legal exposure for lenders in order to make the default sticky. Under our plan, lenders would have stronger incentives to provide meaningful disclosures to those whom they convince to opt out, because they would face increased regulatory scrutiny, or increased costs if the loans did not work out.

Future work will need to explore in greater detail the enforcement mechanism. For example, under one potential approach to making the opt-out sticky, if default occurs when a borrower opts out, the borrower could raise the lack of reasonable disclosure as a defense to bankruptcy or foreclosure. Using an objective reasonableness standard akin to that used for warranty analysis under the Uniform Commercial Code, if the court determined that the disclosure would not effectively communicate the key terms and risks of the mortgage to the typical borrower, the court could modify or rescind the loan contract.[8] Another alternative would be to have the banking agencies (or another expert consumer agency) enforce the requirement on a supervisory basis, rather than relying on the courts. The agency would be responsible for supervising the nature of disclosures according to a reasonableness standard, and would impose a fine on the lender and order corrective actions if the disclosures were found to be unreasonable. The precise nature of the stickiness required and the tradeoffs involved in imposing these costs on lenders would need to be explored in greater detail, but in principle, a sticky opt-out policy could effectively leverage the behavioral insight that defaults matter with the industrial-organizational insight that certain market incentives work against a pure opt-out policy.

An opt-out mortgage system with stickiness might provide several benefits over current market outcomes. Under the plan, a plain-vanilla set of default mortgages would be easier to compare across mortgage offers. Information would be more efficiently transmitted across the market. Consumers would be likely to understand the key terms and features of such standard products better than they would alternative mortgage products. Price competition would more likely become salient once features are standardized. In behavioral terms, when alternative products are introduced, consumers would be made aware that such alternatives represent deviations from the default, helping to anchor consumers in the terms of the default product and providing some basic expectations for what ought to enter into their choices. Framing the mortgage choice as one between accepting a standard mortgage offer and needing affirmatively to choose a nonstandard product should improve consumer decision making. Creditors will be required to make heightened disclosures about the risks of the alternative loan products for the borrower, subject to legal sanction in the event of failure to reasonably disclose such risks; the legal sanctions should deter creditors from making highly unreasonable alternative offers with hidden and complicated terms. Consumers may be less likely to make significant mistakes. In contrast to a pure product regulation approach, the sticky default approach would allow lenders to continue to develop new kinds of mortgages, but only when they can adequately explain key terms and risks to borrowers.

Moreover, requiring a default to be offered, accompanied by required heightened disclosures and increased legal exposure for deviations, may help to make high-road lending more profitable than low-road lending—at least if deviations resulting in harm are appropriately penalized. If offering an opt-out mortgage product helps to split the market between high- and low-road firms, and rewards the former, the market may shift (back) toward firms that offer home mortgage products that better serve borrowers. For this to work effectively, the default— and the efforts to make the default sticky—would need to enable the consumer easily to distinguish the typical "good" loan, benefiting both lender and borrower, and which would be offered as the default, from a wide range of "bad" loans: for example, those that benefit the lender with higher rates and fees but harm the borrower; those that benefit the borrower but harm the lender; and those that harm the borrower and lender but benefit third parties, such as brokers.

There will be costs associated with requiring an opt-out home mortgage. For example, the sticky defaults may not be sticky enough to alter outcomes, given market pressures. The default could be undermined, as well, through the firm's incentive structures for loan officers and brokers, which could provide greater rewards for nonstandard loans. Implementation of the measure may be costly and the disclosure requirement and uncertainty regarding enforcement of the standard might reduce overall access to home mortgage lending. There may be too many cases in which alternative products are optimal, so that the default product is in essence "incorrect," and comes to be seen as such. The default would then matter less over time, and forcing firms and consumers to go through the process of deviating from it would become increasingly just another burden (like existing disclosure paperwork) along the road to getting a home mortgage loan. Low-income, minority, or first-time homeowners who have benefited from more flexible underwriting and more innovative mortgage developments might see their access reduced if the standard set of mortgages does not include products suitable to their needs.

We could improve these outcomes in a variety of ways. For example, the opt-out regulation could require that the standard set of mortgages include a thirty-year fixed mortgage, a five- or seven-year adjustable-rate mortgage, and straightforward mortgages designed to meet the particular needs of first-time, minority, or low-income homeowners. We might develop "smart defaults," based on key borrower characteristics, such as income and age. With a handful of key facts, an optimal default might be offered to an individual borrower. The optimal default would consist of a mortgage or set of mortgages that most closely align with the set of mortgages that the typical borrower with that income, age, and education would prefer. For example, a borrower with rising income prospects might appropriately be offered a five-year adjustable-rate mortgage. Smart defaults might reduce error costs associated with the proposal and increase the range of mortgages that can be developed to meet the needs of a broad range of borrowers, including lower-income or first-time homeowners; however, smart defaults may add to consumer confusion. Even if the consumer (with the particular characteristics encompassed by the smart default) only faces one default product, spillover from too many options across the market may make decision making more difficult. Moreover, it may be difficult to design smart defaults consistent with fair lending rules.

Another approach to improve the standard mortgage choice set and to reduce enforcement costs over time would be to build in banking agency supervision as well as periodic required reviews of the defaults, with consumer experimental design or survey research to test both the products and the disclosures, so that the disclosures and the default products stay current with updated knowledge of outcomes in the home mortgage market. Indeed, lenders might be required to conduct such research and to disclose the results to regulators and the public upon developing a new product and its related disclosures. In addition, regulators might use the results of the research to provide safe harbors for disclosures that are shown to be reasonable ex ante through these methods. Regulators could also issue "no-action" letters regarding disclosures that are deemed to be reasonable through such research. The appropriate federal and state supervisory agencies could be required to conduct ongoing supervision and testing of compliance with the opt-out regulations and disclosure requirements. The federal and state banking agencies could easily adapt to this additional role with respect to depositories, while the FTC, a new expert consumer finance agency, or state agencies would need to be provided with the authority and resources to conduct ongoing supervisory and testing functions for nondepositories, instead of relying solely on enforcement actions. Through these no-action letters, safe harbors, supervision, and other regulatory guidance, the regulators can develop a body of law that would increase compliance across the diverse financial sectors involved in mortgage lending, while reducing the uncertainty facing lenders from the new opt-out requirement, and providing greater freedom for financial innovation.

Restructure the Relationship Between Brokers and Borrowers

An alternative approach to addressing the problem of market incentives to exploit behavioral biases would be to focus directly on restructuring brokers' duties to borrowers and reforming compensation schemes that provide incentives to brokers to mislead borrowers. Mortgage brokers have dominated the subprime market. Brokers generally have been compensated with "yield spread premiums" (YSPs) for getting borrowers to pay higher rates than those for which the borrower would qualify. Such YSPs have been used widely.[9] In loans with yield spread premiums, unlike other loans, there is wide dispersion in prices paid to mortgage brokers. As Howell Jackson has shown, within the group of borrowers paying yield spread premiums, African Americans paid $474 more for their loans, and Hispanics $590 more, than white borrowers; thus, even if minority and white borrowers could qualify for the same rate, in practice minority borrowers are likely to pay much more.[10]

Brokers cannot be monitored sufficiently by borrowers (*see* Jackson and Burlingame 2007), and it is dubious that additional disclosures would help borrowers be better monitors (*see*, for example FTC 2007), in part because brokers' disclosures of potential conflicts of interest may paradoxically increase consumer trust (Cain *et al* 2005). Thus, if the broker is required to tell the borrower that the broker works for himself, not in the interest of the borrower, the borrower's trust in the broker may increase—after all, the broker is being honest! Moreover, evidence from the subprime mortgage crisis suggests that while in theory creditors and investors have some incentives to monitor brokers, they do not do so effectively.

It is possible to undertake an array of structural changes regarding the broker-borrower relationship. For example, we could alter the incentives of creditors and investors to monitor mortgage brokers by changing liability rules to make it clear that broker misconduct can be attributed to lenders and creditors in suits by borrowers (*see* Engel and McCoy 2007). We could directly regulate mortgage brokers through licensing and registration requirements (as is done elsewhere; for example, in the U.K.); recent U.S. legislation now mandates licensing and reporting requirements for brokers. In addition, the ex post disclosure standard we suggest might have a salutary effect by making it more costly for lenders when brokers evade disclosure duties; this may lead to better monitoring of brokers.

We also believe it is worth considering fundamentally altering the duties of brokers by treating mortgage brokers as fiduciaries *to borrowers,* and subjecting them to requirements similar to those that govern investment advisors under the Investment Advisors Act. This would, of course, require vast changes to the brokerage market, including to the ways in which mortgage brokers are compensated, and by whom. We would need to shift from a lender-compensation system to a borrower-compensation system, and we would need a regulatory system and resources to police the fiduciary duty. An interim step with much lower costs, and potentially significant benefits, would be to ban yield spread premiums. Banning YSPs could reduce some broker abuses by eliminating a strong incentive for brokers to seek out higher-cost loans for customers. In fact, quite recently a number of lenders have moved away from YSPs to fixed fees with some funds held back until the loan has performed well for a period of time, precisely because of broker conflicts of interest in seeking higher YSPs rather than sound loans. Banning YSPs now would reinforce these high-road practices and protect against a renewed and profitable low-road push for using YSPs to increase market share once stability is restored to mortgage markets. Banning YSPs would constitute a form of scoring change, corresponding to regulation in the bottom right of table 2, because it affects the payoff brokers receive for pursuing different mortgage outcomes.

III.2 Behaviorally Informed Credit Card Regulation

Using Framing and Salience in Disclosures to Encourage Good Credit Card Behavior

Credit card companies have fine-tuned product offerings and disclosures in a manner that appears to be systematically designed to prey on common psychological biases—biases that limit consumer ability to make rational choices regarding credit card borrowing.[11] Behavioral economics suggests that consumers underestimate how much they will borrow and overestimate their ability to pay their bills in a timely manner.[12] Credit card companies can then price their credit cards and compete on the basis of these fundamental human failings.[13] Nearly 60 percent of credit card holders do not pay their bills in full every month (Bucks *et al* 2006). Moreover, excessive credit card debt can lead to personal financial ruin. Credit card debt is a good predictor of bankruptcy.[14] Ronald Mann has argued that credit card companies seek to keep consumers in a "sweat box" of distressed credit card debt, paying high fees for as long as possible before finally succumbing to bankruptcy.[15]

The 2005 bankruptcy legislation[16] focused on the need for improved borrower responsibility but paid insufficient attention to creditor responsibility for borrowing patterns. Credit card companies provide complex disclosures regarding teaser rates, introductory terms, variable rate cards, penalties, and a host of other matters. Both the terms themselves and the disclosures are confusing to consumers.[17] Credit card companies are not competing, it appears, to offer the most transparent pricing.

Going forward, regulatory and legislative steps could help prod the credit card industry into better practices. The Office of the Comptroller of the Currency intervened to require national banks to engage in better credit card practices and to provide greater transparency on minimum payments,[18] and the Federal Reserve recently released proposed changes to its regulations under TILA, in part in the wake of TILA amendments contained in the bankruptcy legislation.[19] Under the proposals, for example, creditors would need to disclose that paying only the minimum balance would lengthen the payoff time and interest paid on the credit card; describe a hypothetical example of a payoff period paying only the minimum balance; and provide a toll-free number for the consumer to obtain an estimate of actual payoff time.[20] Although the very length and complexity of the board's proposal hints at the difficulty of the task of using complex disclosure to alter consumer understanding and behavior, such improved disclosures might nevertheless help.

But we could do much better. Congress could require that minimum payment terms be accompanied by clear statements regarding how long it would take, and how much interest would be paid, if the customer's *actual* balance were paid off only in minimum payments, and card companies could be required to state the monthly payment amount that would be required to pay the customer's actual balance in full over some reasonable period of time, as determined by regulation. These tailored disclosures use framing and salience to help consumers, whose intuitions regarding compounding and timing are weak, to make better-informed payment choices based on their specific circumstances. Such an approach would correspond to changing the rules in order to de-bias consumers with behaviorally informed information disclosure, in the top right of table 2. Although credit card companies have opposed such ideas in the past, disclosures based on the customer's actual balances are not overly burdensome.

Disclosures regarding the expected time to pay off actual credit card balances are designed to provide a salient frame intended to facilitate more optimal behavior. But such disclosures may not be strong enough to matter. The disclosures are geared toward influencing borrowers' intention to alter their behavior; however, even if the disclosure succeeds in shaping intention, we know that there is often a large gap between intention and action (Buehler *et al* 2002; Koehler and Poon 2005). In fact, borrowers would need to change behavior in the face of strong inertia and marketing by credit card companies propelling them to make no more than minimum payments. More generally, once such disclosure requirement were enacted, market players opposed to them would promptly attempt to undermine them with countervailing marketing and other policies.

An Opt-Out Payment Plan for Credit Cards

A more promising approach, geared more directly toward shaping behavior rather than influencing intentions, would be to develop an "opt-out payment plan" for credit cards, under which consumers would be required automatically to make the payment necessary to pay off their existing balance over a relatively short period of time unless the customer affirmatively opted out of such a payment plan and chose an alterative payment plan with a longer (or shorter) payment term.[21] Such an approach corresponds to changing the rules through opt-out policies, as in the top right of table 2. Given what we know about default rules and framing, such a payment plan may be followed by many consumers. The payment plan would create expectations about consumer conduct and in any event inertia would cause many households simply to follow the plan. Increasing such behavior would mean lower rates of interest and fees paid, and lower incidence of financial failure. In any event, confronting an optimal payment plan may force cardholders to confront the reality of their borrowing, and this may help to alter their borrowing behavior, or their payoff plans. Moreover, credit card industry players would find it difficult to argue publicly against reasonable opt-out payment plans and, in the face of such plans, to continue using a pricing model based on borrowers going into financial distress.

Of course, an opt-out payment plan will impose costs. Some consumers who, in the absence of the opt-out payment plan, would have paid off their credit cards much faster than the plan provides, might now follow the slower payment plan offered as the default, thus incurring higher costs from interest and fees, and possibly even facing a higher chance of financial failure. Alternatively, some consumers might follow the opt-out payment plan when it is unaffordable for them, consequently reducing necessary current consumption such as medical care or sufficient food, or incurring other costly forms of debt. While there are undoubtedly problems with such an approach, public debate over the proposal would at least have the virtue of engaging all relevant players in an important conversation about fundamental changes in market practice.

Regulate Late Fees

A narrower intervention based on behavioral insights about credit card customers would seek to change the behavior of credit card firms rather than consumers. One problem with the pricing of credit cards is that credit card firms can charge late and overlimit fees with relative impunity because consumers typically do not believe ex ante that they will pay such fees. In principle, firms need to charge late and overlimit fees to the extent that they wish to provide incentives to customers not to pay late or go over their credit card limits. In practice, given the fees they charge, credit card firms are perfectly content to let consumers pay late and go over their card limits, in order to obtain fee revenue from them.

We would change the scoring of the game (corresponding to a regulatory choice in the bottom right of table 2). Under our proposal, firms could deter consumers from paying late or going over their credit card limits with whatever fees they deemed appropriate, but the bulk of such fees would be placed in a public trust to be used for financial education and assistance to troubled borrowers. Firms would retain a fixed percentage of the fees to pay for their actual costs incurred from late payments or overlimit charges, or for any increased risks of default that such behavior presages. The benefit of such an approach is that it permits firms to deter "bad conduct" by consumers, but prevents firms from taking advantage of the psychological insight that consumers predictably misforecast their own behavior with respect to paying late and borrowing over their limit. Firm incentives to overcharge for late payments and overlimit borrowing would be removed, while firms would retain incentives appropriately to deter these consumer failures.

As with our other proposals, there would be costs as well: in particular, the reduced revenue stream to lenders from these fees would mean that other rates and fees would be adjusted to compensate, and there is little reason to believe that the adjustments would be in consumers' favor. Moreover, taxing late and overlimit fees in this manner might be seen as a significant interference with contractual relationships beyond the form and content of disclosures required under TILA for credit card agreements.

Opt-Out Credit Card

As a last option to consider in the credit card market, we might think about a regulation requiring firms to offer a standard opt-out credit card. Elizabeth Warren (2007) has argued that private sector firms should offer "clean" credit cards with straightforward terms and honest pricing. We agree with her that this would be a significant achievement and would set an important example for others. Looking at the structure of the market, we might wonder whether such a high-road firm offering a clean credit card could win market share and remain profitable. Given predictable consumer biases, such firms will have a hard time competing with low-road players offering less transparent and seemingly "better" offers. We thus wonder whether regulation might be designed to reward high-road credit card firms while penalizing low-road firms offering products designed to take advantage of consumer failings.

Warren's innovative suggestion in this regard is for the creation of a consumer financial safety commission that could review credit card offers.[22] Perhaps an entity such as this could specify terms and conditions that are "safe" and qualify for being offered as a standard credit card. As with the home mortgage idea discussed earlier, consumers would be offered credit cards that meet the definition of "safe." They could opt for another kind of credit card, but only after meaningful disclosure. And credit card firms would face increased liability risk if the disclosure were found to have been unreasonable. As with our earlier concept, the precise details of liability determination and consequences would need to be carefully calibrated. In essence, the proposal would permit firms to continue to innovate in credit card practices, but with strong pressure to adopt straightforward practices and with the risk of increased consequences to firms when consumers opt out and wind up in trouble. This type of sticky opt-out provision, as with our proposal for an opt-out home mortgage, would correspond to changing both the rules and the scoring of the game on the right side of table 2.

III.3 Increasing Saving Among LMI Households

Savings is an area ripe for further behavioral attention. So far, much of behaviorally informed saving policy has focused on using defaults to improve retirement saving. For many low- and moderate-income households, however, there is a much greater need to focus on basic banking services and short-term savings options, services which, for this population, may require a different mix of governmental responses than those envisioned in the context of retirement savings for middle- and upper-income households.

Many low- and moderate-income (LMI) individuals lack access to the sort of financial services that middle-income families take for granted, such as checking accounts or easily utilized savings opportunities. High-cost financial services, barriers to savings, lack of insurance, and credit constraints increase the economic challenges faced by LMI families. In the short run, it is often hard for these families to deal with fluctuations in income that occur because of job changes, instability in hours worked, medical illnesses or emergencies, changes in family composition, or myriad other factors that can cause abrupt changes in economic inflows and outflows. At low income levels, small income fluctuations may create serious problems in paying rent, utilities, or other bills. Moreover, the high costs and low utility of the financial transaction services used by many low-income households extract a daily toll on take-home pay. Limited access to mainstream financial services reduces ready opportunities to save and thus limit families' ability to build assets and to save for the future.

In theory, opt-out policies ought to work well here, as in the retirement world, in encouraging saving by such households. However, while in general the market pulls in the same direction as policy for saving, market forces weaken or break down entirely with respect to encouraging saving for low-income households. This is simply because the administrative costs of collecting small-value deposits are high in relation to banks' potential earnings on the relatively small amounts saved, unless the bank can charge high fees; with sufficiently high fees, however, it is not clear that having a bank account makes economic sense for LMI households. Indeed, the current structure of bank accounts is one of the primary reasons why LMI households do not have them.

With respect to transaction accounts, high minimum-balance requirements, high fees for overdraft protection or bounced checks, and delays in check clearance dissuade LMI households from opening or retaining bank accounts. Moreover, banks use the private ChexSystems to screen out households who have had difficulty with accounts in the past. Behaviorally insightful tweaks are unlikely to suffice in this context; rather, we need to devise methods to change the nature of the products being offered and, with them, the behavior of the consumers who open and maintain the accounts.

In this area, we need to figure out how to increase scale and offset costs for the private sector, in addition to increasing saving by low- and moderate-income families. As explained more fully below, we propose two options: a new tax credit to financial institutions for offering safe and affordable bank accounts, and a proposal under which the IRS would direct deposit tax refunds into "opt-out" bank accounts automatically set up through private sector financial institutions at tax time. Both proposals are designed to induce the private sector to change their account offerings by offering tax subsidies or government bundling to reach scale, as well as to alter consumer behavior through the structure of the accounts offered. The proposals pertain to changing the rules and the scoring on the left hand side of table 2, where markets may prove neutral to, or even positively inclined toward, the potential overcoming of consumer fallibility. In particular, the tax credit and government backing change the scoring to firms for offering such products, while the opt-out nature of the proposal changes the starting rules.

Tax Credit to Financial Institutions for
Offering Safe and Affordable Bank Accounts

To overcome the problem of the high fixed costs of offering sensible transaction accounts to low-income individuals with low savings levels, Congress could enact a pay-for-performance tax credit for financial institutions that offer safe and affordable bank accounts to LMI households (*see* Barr 2004, 2007). With such a tax credit, financial institutions would be entitled to claim tax credits for a fixed amount per account opened by LMI households. The bank accounts eligible for the tax credit could be structured and priced by the private sector, but according to essential terms required by regulation. For example, costly and inefficient checking accounts with high risk of overdraft or costly hidden features would be eschewed in favor of low-cost, low-risk accounts with only debit-card access. In particular, bank accounts would be debit-card based, with no check-writing capability, no overdrafts permitted, and no ChexSystems rejections for past account failures, in the absence of fraud or other meaningful abuse.

The power of the tax credit initiative could be significantly increased if it were coupled with a series of behaviorally informed efforts to improve take-up of the accounts and savings outcomes for account holders. For example, banks could reach out to employers to encourage direct deposit and automatic savings plans to set up default rules that would increase savings outcomes. With an automatic savings plan, accounts could be structured so that holders could designate a portion of their paycheck to be deposited into a savings "pocket"; the savings feature would rely on the precommitment device of automatic savings, and funds would be somewhat more difficult to access than those in the regular bank account, in order to make the commitment more likely to stick. To provide necessary access to emergency funds in a more cost effective manner than usually available to LMI households, the bank account could also include a six-month consumer loan with direct deposit and direct debit, using relationship banking and automated payment systems to provide an alternative to costly payday loans. With direct deposit of income and direct debit of interest and principal due, the loan should be relatively costless to service and relatively low-risk for the bank. With a longer payment period than usual for payday lending, the loan should be more manageable for consumers living paycheck to paycheck, and would likely lead to less repeated borrowing undertaken to stay current on past payday loans. Moreover, the loan repayment features could also include a provision that consumers "pay themselves first," by including a savings deposit to their account with every payment. Such a precommitment device could overcome the tendency to procrastinate in savings and reduce the likelihood of needing future emergency borrowing. All these efforts could increase take-up of the banking product and lead to improved savings outcomes.

An Opt-Out Bank Account for Tax Refunds

Congress could also enact a new, opt-out "tax refund account" plan to encourage savings and expanded access to banking services, while reducing reliance on costly refund loans (*see* Barr 2007). Under the plan, unbanked low-income households who file their tax returns would have their tax refunds directly deposited into a new account. Banks agreeing to offer safe and affordable bank accounts would register with the IRS to offer the accounts, and a fiscal agent for the IRS would draw from a roster of banks offering these services in the taxpayer's geographic area in assigning the new accounts. On receiving the account number from its fiscal agent, the IRS would directly deposit EITC (and other tax refunds) into those accounts. Taxpayers could choose to opt out of the system if they did not want to directly deposit their refund, but we would expect the accounts to be widely accepted since they would significantly reduce the costs for taxpayers of receiving their tax refunds. Once the tax refund account is set up through the IRS mechanism at tax time, households would receive their tax refund in the account, weeks earlier than if they had to wait for a paper check. Moreover, once it is established, the account could continue to be used long past tax time. Households could also use the account just like any other bank account—to receive their income, to save, to pay bills, and the like.

By using an opt-out strategy and reaching households at tax time, this approach could help to overcome consumer biases to procrastinate in setting up accounts. By reducing the time it takes to receive a refund, setting up such accounts could help to reduce the incentives to take out costly refund loans, incentives that are magnified by temporal myopia and widespread misunderstanding of the costs of credit. This system could dramatically, efficiently, and quickly reach millions of LMI households and bring them into the banking system. A complementary approach (Koide 2007) would reach sufficient scale by using prepaid debit cards and pooled accounts offered by a single vendor chosen by the IRS, rather than individual bank accounts offered by a large number of financial institutions. In this manner, the private sector vendor would be assured a large scale of operations. In either event, opt-out strategies and government incentives would be coupled to reach low-income households with essential banking services.

IV. Concluding Remarks

We propose a different approach to regulation. Whereas the classical perspective assumes that people generally know what is important and knowable, plan with insight and patience, and carry out their plans with wisdom and self-control, the central gist of the behavioral perspective is that people often fail to know and understand things that matter; that they misperceive, misallocate, and fail to carry out their intended plans; and that the context in which people function has great impact on their behavior, and, consequently, merits careful attention and constructive work. In our framework, successful regulation requires integrating this richer view of human behavior with our understanding of markets. Firms will operate on the contour defined by this psychology and will respond strategically to regulations. As we describe above, because firms have a great deal of latitude in issue framing, product design, and so on, they have the capacity to affect behavior and circumvent or pervert regulatory constraints. Ironically, firms' capacity to do so is *enhanced* by their interaction with "behavioral" consumers (as opposed to the hypothetically rational actors of neoclassical economic theory), since so many of the things a regulator would find very hard to control (for example, frames, design, complexity, etc.) can greatly influence consumers' behavior. The challenge of behaviorally informed regulation, therefore, is to be well designed and insightful both about human behavior and about the behaviors that firms are likely to exhibit in response to both consumer behavior and regulation.

With that in mind, we have outlined ten ideas: (1) full information disclosure to de-bias home mortgage borrowers; (2) a new standard for truth in lending; (3) a "sticky" opt-out home mortgage system; (4) restructuring the relationship between brokers and borrowers; (5) using framing and salience to improve credit card disclosures; (6) an opt-out payment plan for credit cards; (7) an opt-out credit card; (8) regulating of credit card late fees; (9) a tax credit for banks offering safe and affordable accounts; and (10) an opt-out bank account for tax refunds. These examples, we hope, will serve to encourage more behaviorally informed regulation in years to come.

Notes

1 For more details, *see*: http://legacy.americanpayroll.org/pdfs/paycard/DDsurv_results0212.pdf.

2 We recognize that there are significant compliance issues regarding pensions and retirement plans, disclosure failures, fee churning and complicated and costly fee structures, conflicts of interest in plan management, as well as problems with encouraging employers to sign up low-wage workers for retirement plans. We do not mean to suggest that these failings are trivial—far from it. We only mean to suggest that, as a comparative matter, market incentives to overcome psychological biases in order to encourage saving are more aligned with optimal social policy than market incentives to exacerbate psychological biases that encourage borrowing.

3 We use this bimodal framework of regulatory choice to simplify the exploration of how our model of individual psychology and firm incentives affects regulation. We acknowledge that the regulatory choice matrix is more complex (*see* Barr 2005).

4 This is largely because of the existing regulatory framework: pension regulation gives employers incentives to enroll lower-income individuals in 401(k) programs. Absent this, it is likely that firms would be happy to discourage enrollment since they often must pay the match for these individuals. This point is interesting because it suggests that even defaults in savings only work because some other regulation "changed the scoring" of the game.

5 This example abstracts from collection costs (which would reduce firms' incentives to hide borrowing costs) and instead focuses on the short-term behavior generally exhibited by firms, as in the recent home mortgage crisis.

6 *See* Federal Reserve Board, Final Rule Amending Regulation Z, 12 CFR part 226 (July 14, 2008); Summary of Findings: Consumer Testing of Mortgage Broker Disclosures, submitted to the Board of Governors of the Federal Reserve System, July 10, 2008; Federal Reserve Board, Proposed Rule Amending Regulation Z, 12 CFR part 226 (June 14, 2007), Federal Register 72, no. 114: 32948; Design and Testing of Effective Truth in Lending Disclosures, Submitted to the Board of Governors of the Federal Reserve System, May 16, 2007.

7 Elizabeth Warren, for example, has proposed a new Financial Product Safety Commission. *See* Warren 2007.

8 A more aggressive approach would be to permit class-action litigation on an affirmative basis. In this paper, we are not yet able to balance the costs of class-action litigation against the benefits of stronger enforcement.

9 See Jackson and Burlingame 2007, p. 127. While in principle yield-spread premiums could permit lenders legitimately to pass on the cost of a mortgage broker fee to a cash-strapped borrower in the form of a higher interest rate rather than in the form of a cash payment, the evidence suggests that yield-spread premiums are in fact used to compensate brokers for getting borrowers to accept higher interest rates, prepayment penalties, and other loan terms.

10 Ibid.: 125; *see also* Guttentag 2000.

11 *See* generally Bar-Gill 2004: 1373.

12 Ibid.: 1395–96.

13 Ibid.: 1394–95.

14 Mann 2006: 60–69.

15 Mann 2007: 375.

16 *See* Bankruptcy Abuse Prevention and Consumer Protection Act of 2005, Pub L. no. 109-8, 119 Stat. 23 (codified at 11 U.S.C. § 101 *et seq* [2005]).

17 *See*, for example U.S. General Accounting Office, "Credit Cards: Increased Complexity in Rates and Fees Heightens the Need for More Effective Disclosures to Consumers," Report 06-929, 2006.

18 *See*, for example, Office of the Comptroller of the Currency, OCC Bull. 2003-1, "Credit Card Lending: Account Management and Loss Allowance Guidance" (2003); Office of the Comptroller of the Currency, OCC Advisory Letter 2004-4, "Secured Credit Cards" (2004), available at http://www.occ.treas.gov/ftp/advisory/2004-4.doc; Office of the Comptroller of the Currency, OCC Advisory Letter 2004-10, "Credit Card Practices" (2004), available at http://www.occ.treas.gov/ftp/advisory/2004-10.doc.

19 *See* press release, Federal Reserve Board, Proposed Amendments to Regulation Z, available at http://www.federalreserve.gov/BoardDocs/Press/bcreg/2007/20070523/default.htm (May 23, 2007).

20 Federal Reserve Board, Proposed Rule, 12 C.F.R. 226, proposed §.7(b)(12), implementing 15 U.S.C. §1637(b)(11).

21 Barr (2007). For a related proposal, *see* Gordon and Douglas 2005 (arguing for an opt-out direct-debit arrangement for credit cards.

22 Ibid.

References

Adkins, Natalie Ross, and Julie L. Ozanne. "The Low Literate Consumer." *Journal of Consumer Research* 32 (2005): 93–105.

Alexander, Gordon J., Jonathan D. Jones, and Peter J. Nigro. "Mutual Fund Shareholders: Characteristics, Investor Knowledge and Sources of Information." *Financial Services Review* 7 (1998): 301–16.

Arkes, Hal Richard, and Catherine Blumer. "The Psychology of Sunk Cost." *Organizational Behavior and Human Decision Processes* 351 (1985): 124–40.

Ausubel, Lawrence M. "The Failure of Competition in the Credit Card Market." *American Economic Review* (March 1991): 50–81.

Bar-Gill, Oren "Seduction by Plastic." *Northwestern University Law Review* 98, no. 4 (2004): 1373–434.

Barr, Michael S. "Banking the Poor." *Yale Journal on Regulation* 21, no. 1 (2004): 121–237.

———. "Modes of Credit Market Regulation." In Nicolas Retsinas and Eric Belsky, eds. *Building Assets, Building Credit*. Washington, DC: Brookings Institution Press, 2005.

———. "An Inclusive, Progressive National Savings and Financial Services Policy." *Harvard Law and Policy Review* 1, no. 1 (2007): 161–84.

Barr, Michael S., Sendhil Mullainathan, and Eldar Shafir. "Behaviorally Informed Financial Services Regulation." White paper. Washington: New America Foundation, 2008.

Bell, David E. "Regret in Decision Making Under Uncertainty." *Operations Research* 30 (1982): 961–81

Benartzi, Shlomo and Richard H. Thaler. "Save More Tomorrow: Using Behavioral Economics to Increase Employee Saving." *Journal of Political Economy* 112, no. 1, 2 (2004): 164–187.

Berry, Christopher. "To Bank or Not to Bank? A Survey of Low-Income Households." Working Paper Series. Cambridge, MA: Joint Center for Housing Studies, 2004.

Bertrand, Marianne, Dean Karlan, Sendhil Mullainathan, Eldar Shafir, and Jonathan Zinman. "What's Advertising Content Worth? Evidence from a Consumer Credit Marketing Field Experiment." (Manuscript, 2008).

Bucks, Brian K., *et al*. "Recent Changes in U.S. Family Finances: Evidence from the 2001 and 2004 Survey of Consumer Finances." Federal Reserve Bulletin A1, 2006. Available at http://www.federalreserve.gov/pubs/bulletin/2006/financesurvey.pdf.

Buehler, Roger, Dale Griffin, and Michael Ross. "Inside the Planning Fallacy: The Causes and Consequences of Optimistic Time Predictions." In Thomas Gilovich, Dale Griffin, and Daniel Kahneman, eds. *Heuristics and Biases: The Psychology of Intuitive Judgment.* Cambridge: Cambridge University Press, 2002.

———. "Exploring the 'Planning Fallacy': Why People Underestimate Their Task Completion Times." *Journal of Personality and Social Psychology* 67 (1994): 366–81.

Cain, Daylain M., George Lowenstein, and Don A. Moore. "The Dirt on Coming Clean: Perverse Effects of Disclosing Conflicts of Interest." *Journal of Legal Studies* 34, no. 1 (2005): 1–25.

Cialdini, Robert B., John T. Cacioppo, Rodney Bassett, and John A. Miller. "Low-ball Procedure for Producing Compliance: Commitment Then Cost." *Journal of Personality and Social Psychology* 36 (1978): 463–476.

Darley, John M., and C. Daniel Batson. "From Jerusalem to Jericho: A study of Situational and Dispositional Variables in Helping Behavior." *Journal of Personality and Social Psychology* 27 (1973): 100–08.

Design and Testing of Effective Truth in Lending Disclosures, Submitted to the Board of Governors of the Federal Reserve System, May 16, 2007.

Engel, Kathleen C. and Patricia A. McCoy. "Turning a Blind Eye: Wall Street Finance of Predatory Lending." *Fordham Law Review* 75 (2007): 2039.

Freedman, Jonathan L., and Scott C. Fraser. "Compliance Without Pressure: The Foot-in-the-Door Technique." *Journal of Personality and Social Psychology* 4 (1966): 195–203.

Federal Trade Commission. "Improving Consumer Mortgage Disclosures: An Empirical Assessment of Current and Prototype Disclosure Forms." Washington, DC: Bureau of Economics Staff Report, Federal Trade Commission, 2007. Available at http://www.ftc.gov/os/007/06/PO25505mortgagedisclosurereport.pdf.

Gordon, Robert, and Derek Douglas. "Taking Charge." *The Washington Monthly*. December 2005.

Gourville, John T., and Dilip Soman. "Payment Depreciation: The Behavioral Effects of Temporally Separating Payments from Consumption." *Journal of Consumer Research* 25 (1998): 160–74.

Guttentag, Jack. "Another View of Predatory Lending." Working Paper 01-23-B. Philadelphia, PA: Wharton Financial Institutions Center, 2000. Available at http://fic.wharton.upenn.edu/fic/papers/01/0123.pdf.

Iyengar, Sheena S., Wei Jiang, and Gur Huberman. "How Much Choice is Too Much: Determinants of Individual Contributions in 401K Retirement Plans." In Mitchell, Olivia S., and Stephen Utkus, eds. *Pension Design and Structure: New Lessons from Behavioral Finance*. Oxford: Oxford University Press, 2004.

Iyengar, Sheena S., and Mark R. Lepper. "When Choice is Demotivating: Can One Desire Too Much of a Good Thing? *Journal of Personality and Social Psychology* 79 (2000): 995–1006.

Jackson, Howell E., and Laurie Burlingame. "Kickbacks or Compensation: The Case of Yield Spread Premiums." *Stanford Journal of Law, Business and Finance* 12, no. 2 (2007): 289–361.

Johnson, Eric J., and Daniel Goldstein. "Do Defaults Save Lives?" *Science* 302 (2003): 1338–339.

Johnson, Eric J., John Hershey, Jacqueline Meszaros, and Howard Kunreuther. "Framing, Probability Distortions, and Insurance Decisions." *Journal of Risk and Uncertainty* 7 (1993): 35–51.

Kahneman, Daniel. "New Challenges to the Rationality Assumption." *Journal of Institutional and Theoretical Economics* 150 (1994): 18–36.

Kahneman, Daniel, and Amos Tversky. "Prospect Theory: An Analysis of Decision Under Risk." *Econometrica* 47 (1979): 263–91.

Kennedy, Duncan. "Cost-Benefit Analysis of Debtor Protection Rules in Subprime Market Default Situations." In *Building Assets, Building Credit*, Nicolas Retsinas and Eric Belsky, eds. Washington, DC: Brookings Institution Press, 2005.

Knetsch, Jack L. "The Endowment Effect and Evidence of Nonreversible Indifference Curves." *American Economic Review* 79 (1989): 1277–284.

Koehler, Derek J., and Connie S. K. Poon. "Self-Predictions Overweight Strength of Current Intentions." *Journal of Experimental Social Psychology* 42, no. 4 (2005): 517–24.

Koide, Melissa. "The Assets and Transaction Account." Washington, DC: New America Foundation, 2007. Available at http://www.newamerica.net/publications/ policy/assets_and_transaction_account.

Lepper, Mark R., David Greene, and Richard E. Nisbett. "Undermining Children's Intrinsic Interest with Extrinsic Reward: A Test of the 'Overjustification' Hypothesis." *Journal of Personality and Social Psychology* 28 (1973): 129–37.

Lichtenstein, Sarah, and Paul Slovic, eds. *The Construction of Preference*. Cambridge, MA: Cambridge University Press (2006).

Loewenstein, George, and Jon Elster, eds. *Choice Over Time*. New York: Russell Sage Foundation, 1992.

Loewenstein, George, and Richard H. Thaler. "Intertemporal Choice." In R. H. Thaler, ed., *The Winner's Curse: Paradoxes and Anomalies of Economic Life*. New York: Free Press, 1992.

Madrian, Brigitte C., and Dennis F. Shea. "The Power of Suggestion: Inertia in 401(k) Participation and Savings Behavior." *Quarterly Journal of Economics*, 116, no. 4 (2001): 1149–187.

Mann, Ronald. *Charging Ahead: The Growth and Regulation of Payment Card Markets*. Cambridge: Cambridge University Press, 2006.

———. "Bankruptcy Reform and the Sweat Box of Credit Card Debt." *University of Illinois Law Review* 2007, no. 1: 375–403.

Milgram, Stanley. *Obedience to Authority*. New York: Harper and Row, 1974.

Musto, David K. "Victimizing the Borrowers: Predatory Lending's Role in the Subprime Mortgage Crisis." Philadelphia, PA: Wharton working paper, 2007. Published February 20, 2008, on Knowledge@Wharton: http://knowledge. wharton.upenn.edu/article.cfm?articleid=1901.

Redelmeier, Donald A., and Eldar Shafir. "Medical Decision Making in Situations That Offer Multiple Alternatives." *Journal of the American Medical Association* 273, no. 4 (1995): 302–305.

Samuelson, William, and Richard J. Zeckhauser. "Status Quo Bias in Decision Making." *Journal of Risk and Uncertainty* 1 (1988): 7–59.

Schultz, Ellen. "Helpful or Confusing? Fund Choices Multiply for Many Retirement Plans." *The Wall Street Journal* (December 22, 1995): C1, C25.

Shafir, Eldar, Itamar Simonson, and Amos Tversky. "Reason-Based Choice." *Cognition* 49 (1993): 11–36.

———. "A Behavioral Perspective on Consumer Protection." *Competition and Consumer Law Journal* 15, no. 3 (2008): 302–17.

Thaler, Richard H. "Mental Accounting and Consumer Choice." *Marketing Science* 4 (1985): 1999–214.

————. *The Winner's Curse: Paradoxes and Anomalies of Economic Life.* New York: Free Press, 1992.

————. "Mental Accounting Matters." *Journal of Behavioral Decision Making* 12, no. 3 (1999): 183–206.

Thaler, Richard H., and Cass R. Sunstein. *Nudge: Improving Decisions About Health, Wealth, and Happiness.* New Haven, CT: Yale University Press, 2008.

Tversky, Amos, and Daniel Kahneman. "Loss Aversion in Riskless Choice: A Reference Dependent Model." *Quarterly Journal of Economics* 106 (1991): 1039–61.

Tversky, Amos, and Eldar Shafir. "Choice Under Conflict: "The Dynamics of Deferred Decision." *Psychological Science* 3 (1992): 358–61.

Warren, Elizabeth. "Unsafe at Any Rate." *DEMOCRACY: A Journal of Ideas* 8 (2007).

White, James J. and Robert S. Summers. *Uniform Commercial Code*, 4th ed. Practitioner Treatise Series. St. Paul, MN: West Publishing, 1995.

CHAPTER 3

From Greenspan's Despair to Obama's Hope: The Scientific Bases of Cooperation as Principles of Regulation

Yochai Benkler

"*Those of us who have looked to the self-interest of lending institutions to protect shareholders' equity (myself especially) are in a state of shocked disbelief.*"
—Written testimony of Dr. Alan Greenspan,
    Committee of Government Oversight and Reform, October 23, 2008

HENRY WAXMAN: *In other words you found that your view of the world, your ideology was not right. It was not working.*

ALAN GREENSPAN: *Precisely, no I, that's precisely the reason I was shocked because I've been going for forty years or more with very considerable evidence that it was working exceptionally well.*
—Committee of Government Oversight and Reform hearing,
    October 23, 2008

"*We have never been just a collection of individuals. . . .*"
—Victory speech of President Barack Obama, November 4, 2008

Morning, November 4, 2008. We're standing in line, my two sons, my wife, and I; waiting to volunteer at the Obama campaign headquarters in Raleigh, North Carolina; waiting to be told how to be useful in this battleground state. We have come down from Cambridge, Massachusetts for the last few days of the campaign, and have met many people. This morning the campaign headquarters is brimming with people, black and white, young and old. A well-turned-out middle-class white woman with a lilting Southern accent is sitting at a phone-bank table next to a young African American student in his early twenties; both are calling people to say, *Go vote!* Voting, the standard rational-actor model would normally say, is irrational. Volunteering: inexplicable. My nine-year-old, on the phone, suddenly lights up—"Yes," he says, "of course I'm real!" The person on the other end of the line is clearly warming to the young voice full of seriousness, and they take obvious pleasure from talking to each other, if only for a few seconds: "I voted," the person seems to say, as Ari smiles broadly and replies, "That's wonderful!" A human connection.

The campaign of candidate Obama—and, if he can convert it into a well-designed, thoughtful practice of governance, the presidency of President Obama—must give us the answer to the questions that all of us looking at the enormous challenges of tomorrow, and specifically at the global economic crisis, must face: How do we think about practical governance now that the model of well-designed incentives for selfish beings has collapsed around us? How do we convert what has inspired millions in the Obama campaign into a practical replacement for the economic model that Alan Greenspan says he has been relying on for forty years, and which has now failed him in the fall of 2008?

The answer is that we already have the building blocks of a new approach to organizing production and consumption, to organizing governance and practical problem solving in both the public and private arenas. It is this approach that is responsible for developing the free and open-source software that runs the vast majority of Web sites and Internet functions we use every day. It is the approach that allowed Toyota to build better and more productive relations with the very same employees and suppliers that General Motors had alienated. It is the approach that has led contemporary evolutionary biology to see cooperation, rather than competition alone, as a fundamental force of evolution. It is the approach that has motivated the rapid spread of community-policing initiatives in the majority of police departments around the country. In none of these cases is the alternative to the self-interest model that animated Greenspan's ideology a starry-eyed reliance on hope, or a generalized belief in human benevolence. Rather, in every case, a carefully designed or organically grown system structures and gives form to a set of basic assumptions very different from Greenspan's: the assumption that a majority of us care not only about ourselves, but also about others with whom we interact and the groups we see ourselves as belonging to; that we care not only about what is in it for us in a given situation (although we care about that too), but also about what is the right and fair thing to do; and that most of us care about the social context we live in, and respond to our understanding of a social situation as social beings, and not merely as a collection of individuals, relentlessly driven to maximize our own returns and to coordinate for our common good only when the incentives are set just right to lead us by the nose to that result.

During the week or so after Alan Greenspan's testimony before Congress, we saw several editorials and comments about behavioral economics, or what some have derisively derided as merely "the economics of stupid people." Behavioral economics mainly studies how people fail to think rationally or to act upon what would theoretically be in their rational self-interest, supposedly because human beings pervasively lack self-discipline. Nonetheless, the discipline's literature would tend to lead policymakers to consider themselves to be somehow immune to this human failing. Rather, legislators, for example, who are influenced by behavioral economics, may flatter themselves that they alone can think clearly, and could set up systems that manipulate the population into doing what their leaders, from an Archimedean standpoint outside the psychological universe of cognitive biases, know is the right outcome for everyone.

However, the key to constructing future regulatory systems does not lie in perfecting the economic theory of how stupid people behave. Nor does it lie in attentive examination of how people make systematic errors in perception and judgment, or experience periodic failures of will. At least, we cannot rely on such studies alone, although they are important. The term in Greenspan's statement that we need to focus on is *self-interest*. If self-interest were the universal motivator, there would be no Wikipedia, no Linux or Apache, or any of the free software applications that run the Internet that we all depend on. If self-interest were the universal motivator, millions of volunteers would not have gone out canvassing for their candidates, nor would they be out in more normal times, serving meals to the homeless, or cleaning up their city parks. If self-interest led to success in business, then it would be Toyota asking for a government handout to help keep it afloat, not General Motors—because it was GM that perfected a production model based on self-interest, as shown in its conflict-ridden negotiations with its unionized employees, in the aggressively competitive bidding that the company has encouraged among its suppliers, and in its incentive compensation schemes for managers that should (according to agency theory, at least) have led to the best management decisions, but plainly did not. By contrast, it was Toyota that took the management-science world by surprise a quarter of a century ago by building a system based on trust, teamwork, and commitment to a set of shared values, instead of trying to perfectly align the self-interest, and only the self-interest, of workers, managers, suppliers, and distributors.

A growing body of work, in disciplines as wide ranging as experimental economics and psychology, human evolutionary biology and neuroscience, and political science, organizational sociology, and management theory, has given us a basis for rejecting, not rationality, but selfishness, as the prime, universal motive of human action. What we find instead, in thousands of experiments and real-world studies, is what we all actually already know from our day-to-day lives: people are not universally selfish. Some are, to be sure. But many, a majority, are not. Many of us care about what happens to others, about doing what is right and fair and appropriate. We care about being trustworthy, and are affected by the social dynamics of the situations in which we find ourselves. The challenge we face is to take what we know from everyday life and from the fact of successful cooperation all around us, combine this knowledge with what are learning at the cutting edge of the social and human sciences, and develop a new model of human action and motivation that will allow us to design cooperative human systems—like Wikipedia and Linux, like Toyota or the community policing movement.

What are the tools that will make up this new approach to cooperative human-systems design? First, a tremendous amount of work is being done in the experimental study of human behavior, mostly in economics and psychology. In these studies, total strangers are brought into laboratory environments where they sit in front of computers and interact with other people, who they typically have never seen, do not see during the experiment, and will never see after the experiment is done. In many of these experiments, people interact with one another in ways that have real economic consequences for them, gaining or losing from a few dollars to (in one experiment) as much as three months' salary. Because the setups are so spare, people are expected to conform as closely as anyone ever would to the predictions of the standard economic models in which Greenspan put such faith. One fact stands out from these studies, above all else: *in no human society examined under controlled conditions have the majority of people consistently behaved like selfish rational actors.* This has been proved true in hundreds of experiments, in more than two dozen countries.

These experiments allow researchers to be very precise in their assumptions about human cooperation, in what they alter under experimental conditions about the nature of social relationships, and in determining what their results might imply. Such experiments gain precision from their reductiveness. Thus a long-term relationship between people might be represented in an experiment by having a pair of people, who are represented to each other only by onscreen icons, repeatedly play a game, ten or even forty times. Participants might be allowed, at most, to spend five minutes face-to-face during a break before going back to sit in front of their computer screens.

Such artificial restrictions create, at most, thin representations of what human relations really are. For this reason, it has been important to enrich experimental studies with real-world observation, which has been undertaken in many different disciplines. Political scientists might look at the Chicago policing and educational systems reforms of the 1990s and 2000s, or they might look at cooperative irrigation systems around the world. Organizational sociologists and management scientists might study the corporate cultures and strategies of different companies to get rich case-based insights into what has worked in the real world. More recently, the Internet has provided us with a breathtaking range of cooperative activities available for study, many of which have generated rich archives, reveal clear paths of relations, and have created a virtual treasure trove of practices allowing us to study what makes cooperation succeed—or fail. Together, these sources of insight, combined with experimental and theoretical work in game theory and evolutionary dynamics that allows us to place our observations in context, are providing us with a powerful set of tools with which to build new systems for human cooperation, systems built on more than a simple mixture of Hobbes's Leviathan—with the strict control hierarchies that his thinking implies—and Adam Smith's invisible hand, with its relentlessly individual incentives-driven focus.

What are the elements of cooperative human-systems design? A useful way of organizing the conclusions of the thousands of articles in many disciplines looking at this question, like the wise men examining an elephant, is to group their findings into core "levers" that encourage cooperation. The literature strongly suggests that attention to each of these levers in the design of human systems will improve the likelihood that a cooperative dynamic will arise and self-stabilize.

Communication

Communication plays a critical role in fostering cooperation. In dozens of experiments, allowing participants to communicate with one another predictably and reliably has led to higher levels of cooperation (Sally 1995). In observational studies too, stabilizing and routinizing communication appears to be a crucial part of the new managerial processes.[1] Focusing on cooperation in the study of human relations is anchored in the tradition of dialogic theories of the self: the idea that the self comes to know its interests, desires, and meaning through communication with others, rather than through solipsistic or egocentric engagement with the self alone. Communication is therefore both a dynamic in its own right, through which people come to see their own goals, preferences, and policies in conversation with others with whom they interact, and a mechanism for achieving the cooperation dynamic in that good communication facilitates most of the other design levers. The effect of communication is a very robust finding in these literatures, and an obvious target for design interventions. It has a large effect in experimental work, and its routinization is one of the core design principles of the organizational shift to collaborative models. In regulatory policy this means, most radically, that the term *communications* in a government agency should not be a euphemism for *propaganda* or *marketing*, but must instead stand for an genuine effort to engage stakeholders and, equally, all citizens, in a conversation about what needs to be done, how, and why.

Situational Framing

We cannot help but think of relations within frames of reference, and these frames in turn shape the remainder of any decision-making process. In sociology, Erving Goffman called this aspect of social interactions "frame analysis" (Goffman 1974). In psychology, it is often called "situational construal" or simply "framing." The baseline phenomenon is the same: we cannot avoid interpreting a situation in which we find ourselves in social and cultural terms. By virtue of the act of interpretation we already at least partly determine the nature of the interaction and our likely behavior in it. This aspect of the interaction is like a lens through which we observe reality; there is no unmediated mechanism giving access to any situation.

One particularly evocative experiment studied whether framing a task by telling the subjects they were playing "the community game" as opposed to telling them that they were playing "the Wall Street game" would make a difference (Liberman *et al* 2004). What the study found was that, with identical payoff structures, when subjects were told they were playing "the community game," about 70 percent opened by cooperating and sustained cooperation for the duration of the experiment, while when subjects were told that they were playing "the Wall Street game," 33 percent opened cooperatively, and the rest "defected" (abandoned cooperative behavior temporarily) and continued to defect throughout the game. The frame in this case may have defined for the test subjects "the right thing to do," or it may have altered their predictions about what the other subjects would do, so as to make cooperation or defection appear to be a better strategy. In any case, the frame clearly had a real effect on behavior of otherwise similar populations encountering otherwise identical payoffs.

Expanded Utility: Empathy and Solidarity

One of the most important ways in which we deviate from pursuing pure self-interest is by caring about others, and caring about the welfare of groups when membership in those groups constitutes at least part of our identity. These emotions are, respectively, empathy and solidarity. One clear experimental finding is that a process of "humanization"—using mechanisms to assure that participants know and recognize the humanity of their counterparts—improves the number of cooperators and the degree of "generosity" they are willing to show others (Bohnet and Frey 1999). Neurological studies support the proposition that agents' brains respond differently to cooperation with humans than to "cooperation" (that is, playing strategies that in game theory count as cooperative) with computers (Rilling *et al* 2002, 2004).

But generally treating other people as human beings worthy of our concern is only one of two signals we give that we consider another worthy of our cooperation or, at least, consider them highly likely to reciprocate. The other major signal we offer to trigger recognition in others that we consider them close to ourselves is the expression of group solidarity. There has been substantial research in social psychology that supports the finding that people increase the degree to which they cooperate with strangers whom they perceive to be part of even very weakly defined solidarity groups. Experimental subjects have long shown greater generosity to and cooperation with others who merely claimed to share their preferences, for example, for paintings by Klee over paintings by Kandinsky (Tajfel and Turner 1979; Yamagishi 1999). Several researchers continue to determine just how minimal the feeling of solidarity must be to trigger cooperation, and to what degree this feeling functions mainly as a heuristic for reciprocity as opposed to an essential constituent of identity with a group (Yamagishi and Mifune 2008).

The role of symbolically marked groups in fostering cooperation is an important field of study in human evolutionary biology, especially in anthropological research on the co-evolution of genes and culture (Boyd 1986, 2004). Moreover, the importance of "affiliation-based trust," in organizational sociology (Zucker 1986) is consistent with the key role of homophily in the formation of social networks (McPherson *et al* 2001), and similar concepts play significant roles in organizational psychology (Haslam 2004). The basic intuition is that either (a) the more people have a sense of being part of a team, or a clan, the more they are willing to sacrifice their own good for the group; or (b) the clearer the "groupness" of the group is to all its members, the more likely that cooperative action by any member will be reciprocated.

Both empathy and solidarity, and their encouragement through face-to-face meetings or detailed descriptions of the background of participants together constitute, then, another important mechanism for the design of human systems. The modern nation-state has a particularly powerful but also ambiguous relationship to group solidarity. At one level, it represents perhaps the most powerful instance of invented solidarity in history, and has proven capable of leading people to great sacrifice. On the other hand, it has also provided the excuse for some of humanity's worst atrocities. As government in particular aims to harness cooperative dynamics, its agencies must be extremely careful in how they deploy appeals to solidarity.

Normativity: Fairness, Rights, and Norm Compliance

In his now classic article "Rational Fools," Amartya Sen emphasizes the importance of what he called "commitment" to human motivation, and the failure of economics, by and large, to account for the possibility that people act out of commitment (Sen 1977). Commitment should cover at least two distinct concerns: what is fair and what is right. And, indeed, a consistent finding of the experimental literature is that fairness is endogenous to the cooperative dynamic. Experimental mechanisms whose designs are based on a selfish-rational-actor model put fairness of outcomes aside, focusing on whether individuals are made better or worse off by a given interaction as a way of predicting their behavior. Likewise, fairness is usually separated in policy analysis from efficiency, and left to be addressed after the desired level of activity has been induced through egocentrically defined incentives. A consistent finding of the experimental literature is that this approach fails to consider that people care about the fair distribution of outcomes, the perceived fairness of the intentions of others, and the fairness of the overall process (Fehr and Schmidt 2003). There is mounting evidence in cognitive psychology and neuroscience supporting the contention that we have both emotional and subconscious cognitive capacity to do what we understand to be moral (Hauser 2006). Government policy that aims to harness cooperative social dynamics must include, as an integral part of the legislative process, public debate about why any new policies are right and fair, and lawmakers must understand that only regulations that those affected believe to be right and fair will be successful.

In addition to seeking to do what is right and fair, we also tend to do what we regard as normal; that is, we conform to social norms (Ellickson 1991; McAdams 1997). Much research into the phenomenon of social conformity has dealt with long-standing, usually tightly knit communities that rely upon many of the "design levers" I describe here. When thinking of design for such recently invented systems as a collaborative wiki, a musician's Web site that seeks voluntary donations, or a process aimed at engaging citizens in supporting a public good (such as recycling or making their homes more energy efficient), social norms must play a different role. At a minimum, they refer not to long-standing internalized norms, but to instances of more or less clearly specified behavioral expectations about what counts as "cooperative" in a given system. Once participants know what counts as cooperation and what counts as failure to cooperate, they can adjust their own actions, as well as judge the actions of others. These expectations function as Schelling coordination norms—arbitrary coordination points that allow people to coordinate their actions without excessive negotiation, such as driving on the left or right, or meeting by the clock in Grand Central Station. Though they lack substantive content, these norms provide focal points for coordinating behavior. Beyond that, they can be explicitly stated expectations about behavior, like those that anchored Wikipedia in its early days and made it unique among cooperative models in being purely norms based. There is evidence that norms that are self-consciously chosen by a group enjoy high adherence with minimal enforcement requirements (Ostrom *et al* 1994). Where these norms evoke background norms that are already culturally ingrained, they may enjoy the status of those already internalized norms, or the norms may themselves be the object of enforcement through another design lever, punishment.

Trust and Authenticity

Trust is the subject of its own immense literature, and the term has been used in many different ways. Often, it has been used to characterize the success of a system that removes the possibility of defection or human error. When used thus, *trust* is not a design lever at all, but rather a description of the outcome of a system, which signifies confidence it its performance. Trust as a design lever should be viewed as a belief that people in a given relationship have about how others in the system will behave when those others may choose to act in ways harmful or helpful to those who trust them (in the absence of genuine choice, the concept of trust has no meaning). It is precisely because trust here refers to an empirical belief people have about the state of the social system within which they act that we treat it as distinct from normativity. *Trust* as I use the term here is not the same as *trustworthiness*. Rather, a system of trust is a system in which people can reasonably hold the belief that some substantial number of others will not take advantage of them whenever they can. A system designed to foster trust in this sense will usually be improved by breaking down cooperative actions into observable steps, so that participants can reduce their vulnerability to one another while observing the proclivities of others to cooperate or defect. A requirement for the creation of trust is that the person constructing the cooperative system act authentically and be seen as acting authentically. Empty promises of community and cooperation may trick others for a short time, but not over the long term. Thus, for example, a government agency that aims to harness cooperation among the citizens with whom it interacts will need to make its commitments to a cooperative dynamic credible, behave in ways that exhibit trustworthiness, and express by its actions trust in citizens.

Transparency and Reputation

Another important design element, the transparency of a system, bears powerfully on the issues of both trust and punishment. Critically, many of the other design features I have discussed depend on participants' knowing who has done what, to and with whom, to what effect, by which mechanism. Recognition of this dependence lies behind the argument that biologists Nowak and Sigmund make about the evolutionary impact of moral accounting (though they do not call it that): such accounting, they suggest, was necessary to sustain indirect reciprocity among our forbears, which in turn may have been the driving force behind the evolution of human intelligence (Nowak and Sigmund 2005). Whether or not they are correct about human evolution, studies in experimental economics typically show that reputation-rich games lead to cooperation more quickly and robustly than anonymous games (Fehr and Gächter 2000). Similarly, reputation systems play a significant role in social-software platforms, ranging from commercial systems such as eBay and Amazon (Resnick and Zeckhauser 2002) to the wide range of commons-based peer-production projects that rely upon the Internet's resources for observing online behavior, building enduring reputations, and influencing opinion.[2] For a government agency, this implies that its internal deliberations and its interactions with interested parties must all be made much more transparent than they typically have been.

Autonomy/Efficacy

There is a significant psychological literature suggesting that people need a personal sense of competence or efficacy in their actions, and pursue activities that satisfy that need (Ryan and Deci 2000). For example, among Toyota's most important reforms of the company's production system was decreasing the number of process engineers and according greater autonomy to teams of employees on the production line (Adler *et al* 1999). The need for autonomy and personal efficacy moreover plays an important role in limiting the efficacy of reward and punishment as complementary, as opposed to competing, means for assuring cooperation. People must not only be assured of their personal autonomy, but the value of their contributions must be recognize before their peers; otherwise, people's incentive to contribute as much as they can is reduced.

Fostering a successful culture of personal autonomy as Toyota has done in the context of government regulation intended to standardize behavior across different contexts is far from trivial. It would require, particularly at the federal level, determining regulatory contexts in which regulators may set relatively broad targets for performance and optimal behavior, and certain excluded categories of intervention, while allowing groups of citizens, (initially municipalities, but in the longer run civil-society organizations and organizations that rely on both public and private funding), to exhibit their competence and to receive authority and funding to achieve a given government goal in a particular context.

Calculation: Punishment, Reward, Crowding Out, and Cost

The design levers discussed above all operate at the level of intrinsic motivations. That is, they all work to induce participants to want to cooperate for reasons that are internal to their own psychological and social needs and desires, rather than in response to external rewards or constraints. However, because both the observational and experimental literature suggest that people vary immensely in their motivations, and that many will inevitably be selfish, stable cooperation systems require some element of external compulsion to keep those who are not driven to cooperate by intrinsic motivations in line. Otherwise cooperation tends to unravel, since the presence of selfish actors may undermine efficacy, fairness, solidarity, or any of the other mechanisms that sustain cooperation even in the presence of defectors.

Mechanisms for disciplining and punishing defectors are therefore important in the design of cooperation platforms. The experimental literature finds that (a) with the right design, reciprocators will usually be willing to incur the cost of punishing defectors in order to keep them in line, without intervention from an external body, such as the state or management, but (b) that punishment can backfire if it is not properly designed (Bowles and Gintis 2002; Fehr and Gächter 2002); Fehr and Rockenbach 2002; Falk 2005). It is important to understand that introducing the idea of punishment does not collapse our analysis back to selfish rationality. Punishment is neither necessary to explain cooperation (we see cooperation without it, most importantly in the "second-order public-goods problem" created by the need to impose costly punishment on defectors) nor sufficient (we see instances in which punishment reduces cooperation, probably through "crowding out"). Indeed, punishment can impose such great costs on groups that it ceases to be worthwhile (Dreber *et al* 2008). Moreover, the degree to which its effects are beneficial or detrimental varies among cultures (Hermann *et al* 2008). Yet punishment is one design lever available to systems designers for improving compliance by selfish actors with the cooperative behavior of the other agents in the system. While punishment has been studied much more extensively, reward systems have a similar structure—participants pay a cost to keep others, who are more self-interested, in line with the common good. In an analytical sense, rewards are merely negative punishments, but rewards have the added benefit of not triggering spirals of negative retaliation.

Considering the ambiguous effects of punishment brings to the fore one more design constraint that has particular importance when government is involved: the phenomenon of crowding out. Crowding out can occur within or among systems. *Intra*system crowding out refers to situations in which the use of one design lever would reduce the efficacy of another. For example, the introduction of punishment may, under certain circumstances, crowd out trust, and thereby undermine, rather than improve, cooperation (Yamagishi 1986). From the psychological literature, we know that rewards too can trigger the crowding-out effect, but not as powerfully, and that they may be susceptible to framing that will induce people to treat them as noncontrolling (Ryan and Deci 2000). *Inter*system crowding out may occur when the designer tries to mix and match elements from cooperative systems with elements from other systems, such as market mechanisms. There is a large literature on crowding out caused by the introduction of money into otherwise cooperation-based interactions (Frey and Jege 2008; Bowles and Gintis 2001). For regulatory systems, crowding out presents a particularly vexing problem, because the body that aims to introduce and foster cooperation is of necessity a body that possesses enormous power, and is typically seen as able to bring coercive power to bear in a relationship. State-based cooperation systems always necessarily involve the risk of some intersystem crowding out; if the state is involved, then citizens may feel that they do not need to contribute, because the state "will take care of it all." On the other hand, the state can structure its role in the cooperative systems it builds as a potentially neutral third-party referee that may moderate the negative effects of punishment where it is needed. This does indeed seem to be precisely the role that impartial justice is supposed to introduce into societies that otherwise might remain plagued by vendetta-like forms of private mutual monitoring, discipline, and punishment.

In addition to punishment and reward, which operate primarily on individuals who otherwise might not cooperate because of their intrinsic drives, it is important to remember that the claims of prosocial motivations do not exclude considerations of personal costs and benefits. The essential conclusion of the literature on cooperation is not that large numbers of us are altruists regardless of cost. Rather, it is that large numbers of us have prosocial motivations—regard for others because of our empathy and solidarity, or regard for the normative implications of what we do, in addition to our other cost-benefit considerations. It is not surprising, therefore, that the cost of cooperation affects its levels and the number of people who cooperate. In experiments, subjects will cooperate more when the cost of doing so is lower, such as when the opportunity cost of cooperating in a prisoner's dilemma is lower because of the payoff structure (Camerer and Fehr 2004). In real life we see peer production online improved when a task has been chunked into sufficiently small modules to make the cost of individual contribution correspondingly small (Benkler 2002).

Social Dynamics

An increasing amount of work being is done today on social networks' effects on behavior. It turns out that, for example, our own obesity is affected by whether our friends and relatives have recently become obese (Christakis and Fowler 2007). While the mechanism is not entirely clear, it appears that there is at least some role played by benchmarking and imitation: that is, we judge our own behavior and outcomes by comparing ourselves to others in our social neighborhood (Hanaki *et al* 2007). Allowing participants to observe each other (transparency) and to form and break attachments selectively with people who are more or less cooperative, so as to increase the number of interactions they have with cooperators as opposed to defectors, is therefore also a valuable feature in human systems design: in this way, groups of cooperators may stabilize and provide mutual support.

One important aspect of social dynamics is leadership. An emphasis on leadership does not emerge from experimental research, which does not examine the phenomenon, but from organizational sociology, where it is a consistent feature (Maccoby and Heckscher 2007). Leadership is emphasized in the study of open-source software (Weber 2005), and repeatedly crops up in field studies of online cooperation as well. It is important to recognize, however, that *leadership* does not necessarily imply *hierarchy*. Rather, what we see in observational research is that people contribute to a given system at many levels. Thus systems need to be designed to accommodate and recognize people's varying patterns of contribution, especially by offering them a voice in the collective governance of the enterprise, or through symbolic means of expressing honor and respect. Moreover, for at least some people, it is precisely the desire to seek positions of power, of leadership, that drives generous, prosocial behavior. The role of gift giving as a modality of asserting dominance, so-called agonistic giving, is widely recognized in the anthropology of the gift,[3] and in fundraising situations in which public exhibition of gifts is a form of asserting status; we also see it in some, but by no means all, online cooperation sites.

The following, then, is a summary of the discussion above as a list of design levers, or design considerations:

- Communication
- Situational framing
- Expanding the utility function:
  - Empathy
  - Solidarity

- Normativity
  - Fairness
  - Moral commitment
  - Norm compliance or conformism
- Trust
  - Trust and authenticity
  - Transparency and reputation
- Autonomy/efficacy
- Calculation
  - Punishment and reward
  - Crowding out
  - Cost
- Social dynamics
  - Social network effects
  - Leadership and asymmetry

No list of fifteen potential design levers can hope to provide the deterministic outcomes implied by simpler models of human motivation and system intervention. For regulators who seek the comfort of a *If you do X, you will increase rewards through action I, and therefore increase the likelihood of outcome O* type of analysis, the work on cooperation will appear too early in its development to provide guidance. However, regulators who understand that human motivation and social, psychological, and cultural interactions are extremely complex phenomena, which cannot be reduced to a simple *If you do X then Y will follow* without enormous loss of information, may be more patient as we try to work out how the design levers nonetheless provide substantial advantages over a mere recognition of the complexity of human action.

Below I will suggest at least an initial set of principles of regulation that would take advantage of the insights of the literature on cooperation, even if we cannot yet provide a deterministic analysis of the desired structure of cooperation-eliciting regulations.

Principles

The design levers provide a framework for thinking about how most effectively to structure cooperative models of solving problems that are the subject of regulation or characterize the regulatory process. To conclude this chapter, I offer five principles of regulation through which regulators may implement the lessons of cooperative dynamics.

1. Develop a capacity for relying on social mechanisms equivalent to the focus in the past quarter century on market mechanisms

One of the dogmas in regulation from the past quarter century has been that government agencies should seek market-based mechanisms to achieve goals previously fulfilled by government. The cooperation literature argues instead for a new focus on cooperative solutions to the problem of providing public goods. This does not mean that cooperative mechanisms will always be best; it does suggest that they are available and sustainable, and that they have different benefits and potential pitfalls from those of either market mechanisms or government-provided services, and should be considered in any given context for their feasibility and relative desirability.

Take for example the peer-to-patent system. Developed by Beth Noveck in collaboration with IBM and the Patents and Trademark Office (PTO), this program attempts to resolve the relative lack of expertise in the patent office in software by opening up software patent applications to a process of peer review. The model relies upon the culture of substantial contribution to the public good that has grown up among software developers, owing to the rise of free and open-source software. Noveck's system invites patent applicants to submit their applications to an expedited review process through which the members of the open community of software developers can look at the application, research potential reasons to preclude patentability, and submit their observations to the patent examiner appointed by the PTO. The point here is not to displace the PTO, but to harness the knowledge of the community and to take advantage of the general willingness to contribute among developers, who are motivated to some degree, to be sure, by competitiveness, but who also are eager to make a difference in the field they care about. Contributors are allowed to submit potential "prior art"—that is, earlier publications or patents that would make the current claim insufficiently novel, or too obvious, to be granted a patent. Others may then annotate and comment on whether the proposed prior art in fact provides good grounds for objecting to the patent, and vote on which are the most likely instances of prior art to effectively limit or entirely invalidate the patent application. The examiner then reviews the top proposed pieces of prior art. My point is not to assert that this system is the best example of harnessing all the design levers to optimize levels of cooperation. Rather, the PTO site provides an example of isolating a particularly sticky regulatory problem and restructuring it in a way that takes advantage of volunteers from the most relevantly affected community to work, together with the government, on implementing a solution.

The more general point is that government agencies must begin to consider engaging citizens in cooperative systems as one potential way to improve aspects of the regulatory process, and also to improve the delivery of services. Today, government lags behind in its capacity to harness social volunteerism to achieve public goods. Compared to the free and open-source software community, which is harnessing volunteer efforts to produce some of the world's most important software, or to civil-society organizations, such as the Sunlight Foundation, which is harnessing volunteer efforts to sift through government accountability-related data to analyze it for evidence of corruption of public officials, government processes have not focused on using their professional staff and public funding to support volunteer efforts that could improve their processes. Agencies need to develop the capabilities, and to offer funding models, that will facilitate the provision of public goods—from skills training in schools and adult educational facilities to the analysis of government corruption—by partnering with market and nonmarket organizations that specialize in harnessing and structuring volunteer efforts, both online and offline.

2. Include in the evaluation of proposed market or command mechanisms expected impact on social provisioning that exists, or that could be constructed as an alternative

It is an unusual characteristic of American society, compared to other major industrial social democracies, that we continue to rely to a much extent greater than they do on volunteer organizations, both religious and secular, to provide social services. In the past, when the market and the state were considered the only possible providers of public goods, our reliance on volunteerism was criticized by some as constituting a partial abdication by the modern social-democratic state of its responsibilities. The contemporary emergence of social production in the networked economy, and the increasing understanding of the possible benefits of sustained social action to provision public goods, places the United States, perhaps paradoxically, at a surprising advantage in making the transition to a new system that would permit greater leeway for social institutions to play a substantial role in serving governmental agencies' purposes.

There is a substantial literature suggesting that government services can sometimes crowd out private volunteerism. The mechanism is not as yet entirely clear: it may be that when a government agency takes over a particular social service, people cease to see providing it as a shared social responsibility—it becomes something we "get from the government"; it may be that there is a loss of the "social-capital value" of contributing, once the contribution is no longer strictly necessary, and volunteering ceases to enhance people's social status; or it may be that when a government agency takes over some social service, volunteers cease to feel motivated, independent, and needed. Whatever the reasons, government action can sometimes undermine social provisioning. Government actions aimed at providing public goods should therefore take into consideration the existing system of providing services, and assess: (a) the presence or absence of a well-functioning social provisioning system for the desired good; (b) the likely effect of the proposed action on that social provisioning; and (c) potential adjustments to the proposed policy that would mitigate the negative effects, if any, on social provisioning. Preferably, government should partner with and support existing social providers.

This principle is, of course, not a hard constraint. There may be other considerations, such as the value placed on the availability of public, nonsectarian sources of provisioning a public good where the only source is sectarian—say, special education or soup kitchens. But the broad principle is clear. Just as in the past proposed government regulations were analyzed to anticipate their interactions with existing and potential market mechanisms, and redesigned to minimize any negative regulatory impact and to take advantage of market mechanisms, so too now, with the newly emerging recognition of the role of social action, government must also consider its effects on the social provisioning of desired public goods, and redesign its programs accordingly.

3. Use network technologies to reconstruct government decision processes to enable effective participation by citizens and affected populations on a continuous basis, including implementation

People tend to follow regulations that they choose themselves more willingly and more observantly than rules set down by a remote other. Improving the actual and perceived level of participation in government regulatory processes will encourage citizens to view new regulations as legitimate, and should also make citizens more likely to view regulations as intrinsically binding. That is, when people participate in making the rules, they are more likely to think that obeying them is the right thing to do, and not something they do merely to avoid censure. A substantial literature already exists on opening up regulatory processes to citizen participation, including sensitive studies of stakeholder participation, on which regulators can now draw. Efforts to reach beyond stakeholders to the citizenry at large have, in the past, been largely treated under the rubric of "eGovernment" and have relied on relatively passive Web 1.0 technologies that allow people with Internet access to read and add comments to Web pages. Such an approach lacks structure, and offers little potential for aggregation of comments and debate among citizens in ways that could render their contributions more salient and politically meaningful.

The next generation of regulators needs to learn from the work on participatory government generally, and adopt processes that will offer the broadest range of citizens a much greater degree of freedom to participate effectively, by submitting comments and commenting on the comments of others, and by collecting and analyzing citizens' preferences to determine their preferences. The Environmental Protection Agency has begun to take steps in this direction; Change.gov began, during the Obama transition, to experiment with ways of increasing citizen's direct participation, such as its house-party discussions of healthcare reform. Beyond these examples, this approach needs to be understood as a new principle of regulation: government must provide the means, both online and offline, for effective, widespread participation by citizens in the regulatory process, from its inception to its conclusion and subsequent oversight.

4. Implement transparency through highly accessible visual interfaces, with capabilities for social observation and commentary on official behavior

Transparency, and the widespread perception that processes are transparent, is essential to cooperation. In earlier times, transparency depended largely on professional auditors and observers—internal government auditors, such as comptrollers, or external independent actors, such as an independent press. Freedom of Information legislation supported this transparency by requiring government agencies to provide information upon request to individuals and nongovernmental organizations. While these elements of transparency are critical, and need to be preserved, current regulatory systems must embrace more radical transparency and more open data communications processes to harness peer production and online social action to the task of assuring that government always operates under the public gaze, that regulatory processes are not hidden from view, and that all the materials involved are available for everyone to examine and analyze. The data that government agencies collect, and records of what they do and how they spend their allocated funds, must be collected and kept up to date; government databases need to be made available for public search and comment; and data needs to be made available in standard formats that will allow civil-society organizations and online unstructured collaborative groups to develop their own open interfaces to it. Only in this way can we harness innovation throughout the network to design ever better platforms for monitoring regulators and holding them accountable.

5. Assess fairness as an integral part of effectiveness

A core finding of the study of cooperation is that people care deeply about fairness, and that their perceptions of the fairness of their interactions have a direct, significant impact on their motivation to participate productively. Fairness should not be mere window dressing for regulations that have efficiency as their main goal. Rather, fairness is essential to stimulate effective, productive engagement by the citizenry in any regulatory process. Fairness is not an ideal, universal state; it is a culturally embedded idea that people in a given society, at a given time, hold about the rewards for their common actions, as well as the intentions and processes involved in determining the distribution of those rewards. Government agencies should develop explicit metrics to assess the impact of their policies. Initially, the focus should be on the distribution of wealth and welfare. The distribution of these social goods should be fully described and measured against a culturally meaningful scale of fair distribution—individually equal (one common measure of fairness in a market-integrated society), progressively redistributive, proportionate to contributions, or based on an articulated theory of desert. These outcomes should be included in the formal analysis of an agency's proposed regulations, and published as part of the regulatory process. Alongside current practices of producing cost-benefit analyses and environmental impact statements, agencies should develop and publicize outcomes-fairness analyses of proposed regulations.

Conclusion

The 1970s, '80s and '90s saw the exquisite refinement of rational-actor theory and used it to justify an ever increasing emphasis on market-based models of regulation and mechanism design. In regulatory practice, this approach became dominant in the Reagan and Thatcher period, and extended its reach with the increasing scope of a European Commission empowered to focus on building an integrated market in what was then called the European Economic Community. The commission therefore emphasized competition and efficiency, and supported institutions of the global trade and monetary system that relied on market-based mechanisms as a matter or principle. Throughout this period a countervailing trend among some scholars advocated more participatory structures, but the global financial crisis of 2008 has brought into the sharpest relief the severe limitations of market-based regulatory approaches. Or at least, the crisis has undermined the nearly absolute dominance that market fundamentalism has had in determining the regulation—or absence of regulation—in financial services.

At the same time, an increasing body of work in the social sciences and particularly in the management and sociology of organizations, as well as on the study of online social practices, has provided substantial new evidence that refines our understanding of the conditions that can sustain forms of social cooperation that are not based on either market mechanisms or command and control. While it is too early to embrace cooperation and collaborative practices as *the* solution to all our regulatory problems, we certainly have enough information and insight to begin to implement regulatory practices that will likely enhance cooperation and the social provision of public goods.

The principles proposed in this essay are intended to orient regulators toward thinking about whether and how they can harness social cooperation to achieve some of the goals that, in the past, they have sought through command and control or through market mechanisms; how their expected actions will affect existing social cooperation, and how core drivers of cooperation in society can be harnessed by focusing on improved participation in, and transparency and fairness of, regulatory processes and outcomes.

Notes

1 *See,* e.g., Anabel Quan-Haase and Barry Wellman, "Hyperconnected Net Work: Computer Mediated Community in a High-Tech Organization," in Heckscher and Adler 2007 (describing communications flows in collaborative segments of a firm).

2 *See,* e.g., "Wikipedia:Barnstars" in Wikipedia: http://en.wikipedia.org/wiki/Wikipedia: Barnstars; or the team-competition contributions in Yochai Benkler, "'Sharing Nicely': On Shareable Goods and the Emergence of Sharing as a Modality of Economic Production," *The Yale Law Journal* 114 (2004): 273.

3 *See,* e.g., Maurice Godelier, *The Enigma of the Gift* (Chicago: University of Chicago Press, 1999).

References

Adler, Paul S., Barbara Goldoftas, and David Levine. "Flexibility Versus Efficiency? A Case Study of Model Changeovers in the Toyota Production System." *Organization Science* 10, no. 1 (1999): 43–68

Benkler, Yochai. "Coase's Penguin, or, Linux and the Nature of the Firm." *The Yale Law Journal* 112, no. 3 (2002): 369–446.

Bohnet, Iris, and Bruno Frey. "The Sound of Silence in Prisoner's Dilemma and Dictator Games." *Journal of Economic Behavior & Organization* 38, no. 1 (1999): 43–57.

Bowles, Samuel. "Policies Designed for Self-Interested Citizens May Undermine 'The Moral Sentiments': Evidence from Economic Experiments." *Science* 320 (2008): 1605–09.

Bowles, Samuel, and Herbert Gintis. "*Homo Reciprocans*: Altruistic Punishment of Free Riders." *Nature* 415 (2002): 125.

Boyd, Robert, and Peter J. Richerson. *Culture and the Evolutionary Process.* Chicago: Chicago University Press, 1986.

————. *Not by Genes Alone: How Culture Transformed Human Evolution.* Chicago: Chicago University Press, 2004.

Camerer, Colin F., and Ernst Fehr. "Measuring Social Norms and Preferences Using Experimental Games: A Guide for Social Scientists." In Joseph Henrich, *et al,* eds. *Foundations of Human Sociality: Economic Experiments and Ethnographic Evidence from Fifteen Small-Scale Societies.* New York: Oxford University Press, 2004.

Christakis, Nicholas A., and James H. Fowler. "The Spread of Obesity in a Large Social Network over 32 Years." *New England Journal of Medicine* 357 (2007): 37–79.

Dreber, Anna, *et al,* "Winners Don't Punish." *Nature* 452 (2008): 348–51.

Ellickson, Robert. *Order Without Law: How Neighbors Settle Disputes.* Cambridge: Harvard University Press, 1991.

Falk, Armin, *et al.* "Driving Forces Behind Informal Sanctions." *Econometrica* 73 (2005): 2017.

Fehr, Ernst, and Simon Gächter. "Cooperation and Punishment in Public Goods Experiments." *American Economic Review* 90, no. 4 (2000): 980–94.

————. "Altruistic Punishment in Humans." *Nature* 415 (2002): 137.

Fehr, Ernst, and Bettina Rockenbach. "Detrimental Effects of Sanctions on Human Altruism, *Nature* 422 (2002): 137.

Fehr, Ernst, and Klaus M. Schmidt. "Theories of Fairness and Reciprocity—Evidence and Economic Applications. Paper prepared for the invited session on Behavioral Economics of the 8th World Congress of the Econometric Society in Seattle, 2000. In Dewatripont, M., *et al,* eds. *Advances in Economics and Econometrics*, Eighth World Congress of the Econometric Society, vol. 1. Cambridge: Cambridge University Press, 2003.

Frey, Bruno S., and Reto Jege. "Motivation Crowding Theory: A Survey of Empirical Evidence." *Journal of Economic Surveys* 15, no. 5 (2001): 589.

Goffman, Erving. *Frame Analysis: An Essay on the Organization of Experience.* New York: Harper & Row, 1974.

Hanaki Nobuyuki, Alexander Peterhansl, Peter S. Dodds, and Duncan J. Watts. "Cooperation in Evolving Social Networks." *Management Science* 53 (2007): 1036–50.

Haslam, S. Alex. *Psychology in Organizations: The Social Identity Approach.* Thousand Oaks, CA: Sage Publications, 2004.

Hauser, Marc. *Moral Minds: How Nature Designed Our Universal Sense of Right and Wrong.* New York: Ecco, 2006.

Heckscher, Charles, and Paul Adler, eds. *The Firm as a Collaborative Community: Reconstructing Trust in the Knowledge Economy.* New York: Oxford University Press, 2007.

Herrman, Benedikt, Christian Thonni, and Simon Gächter. "Antisocial Punishment Across Societies." *Science* (2009) 316: 1362.

Liberman, Varda, Steven M. Samuels, and Lee Ross. "The Name of the Game: Predictive Power of Reputations versus Situational Labels in Determining Prisoner's Dilemma Game Moves." *Personality and Social Psychology Bulletin* 30, no. 9 (2004): 1175–85.

McAdams, Richard. "The Origin, Development, and Regulation of Norms." *Michigan Law Review* 96, no. 338 (1997): 338–433.

McPherson, Miller, Lynn Smith-Lovin, and James Cook. "Birds of a Feather: Homophily in Social Networks." *Annual Review of Sociology* 27 (2001): 415–44.

Maccoby, Michael, and Charles Heckscher. "A Note on Leadership for Collaborative Community." In Heckscher 2007 (see above).

Krueger, Joachim I., and Theresa E. DiDonato. "Social Categorization and the Perception of Groups and Group Differences." *Compass: Social and Personal Psychology* 2 (forthcoming 2008): 1–18.

Nowak, Martin, and Karl Sigmund. "Evolution of Indirect Reciprocity." *Nature* 437 (2005): 1291–98.

Ostrom, Elinor, Roy Gardner, and James Walker. *Rules, Games, and Common Pool Resources.* Ann Arbor: University of Michigan Press, 1994.

Resnick, Paul, and Richard Zeckhauser. "Trust Among Strangers in Internet Transactions: Empirical Analysis of eBay's Reputation System." In *The Economics of the Internet and E-Commerce.* Michael R. Baye, ed. Advances in Applied Microeconomics, vol. 11. Amsterdam: Elsevier Science, 2002.

Rilling, James K., *et al.* "A Neural Basis for Social Cooperation." *Neuron* 35, no. 2 (2002): 395–405.

———. "Opposing Bold Responses to Reciprocated and Unreciprocated Altrusim in Putative Reward Pathways." *Neuroreport* 15, no. 6 (2004): 2539–543.

Ryan, Richard M., and Edward L. Deci. "Self-determination Theory and the Facilitation of Intrinsic Motivation, Social Development, and Well-Being." *American Psychologist* 55 (2000): 68–78.

Sally, David. "Conversation and Cooperation in Social Dilemmas." *Rationality and Society* 7, no. 1 (1995): 57–92.

Sen, Amartya. "Rational Fools: A Critique of the Behavioral Foundations of Economic Theory." *Philosophy and Public Affairs* 6, no. 4 (1977): 317–44.

Tajfel, Henri, and Turner, John. C. "An Integrative Theory of Intergroup Conflict." In W. G. Austin and S. Worchel, eds. *The Social Psychology of Intergroup Relations.* Monterey, CA: Brooks-Cole, 1979.

Yamagishi Toshio. "The Provision of a Sanctioning System as a Public Good." *Journal of Personality Social Psychology* 51 (1986): 110–16.

———. "Generalized Reciprocity and Culture of Collectivism." *Organizational Science* 33, no. 1 (1999): 24–34. (In Japanese.)

Yamagishi Toshio and Mifune Nobuhiro. "Does Shared Group Membership Promote Altruism? Fear, Greed, and Reputation." *Rationality and Society* 20 (2008): 5–30.

Weber, Steve. *The Success of Open Source.* Cambridge: Harvard University Press, 2005.

Zucker, Lynn G. "The Production of Trust: Institutional Sources of Economic Structure, 1840–1920." In Barry M. Staw and L. L. Cummings, eds. *Research in Organizational Behavior*, vol. 8. Greenwich, CT: JAI Press, 1986.

CHAPTER 4

Government as Risk Manager[1]

Tom Baker and David Moss

On Friday, July 11, 2008, after a run on IndyMac Bancorp in which people lined up outside the bank's branches and withdrew $100 million per day, the U.S. Federal Deposit Insurance Corporation seized IndyMac. The next Monday, July 14, IndyMac reopened its branches for business under FDIC supervision. The lines were gone. IndyMac employees largely remained in place. Depositors had immediate access to their funds up to the federally insured amount—$100,000 per person in ordinary accounts and $250,000 per person in retirement accounts—and the FDIC began the slow process of winding up the bank. The deposit insurance system had worked to protect depositors and maintain confidence in the banking system, preventing the type of mass banking panic that crippled the American financial system in the early 1930s.

While there are many parallels between the current financial crisis and the onset of the Great Depression, deposit insurance has made this fundamental difference. There are other differences as well. We have unemployment insurance, along with Social Security, Medicare, Medicaid, and state insurance guaranty funds. People who lose their jobs will receive income replacement benefits for at least some period, and the infrastructure is in place to extend those benefits if necessary. The elderly and the disabled will have a basic income, good health insurance, and basic long-term-care insurance, regardless of what happens to their private retirement plans or other investments. In addition, the state insurance guaranty funds provide protection for insurance products similar to that provided by the FDIC for bank deposits. None of these programs existed in 1930. They will not eliminate the dislocation from the bursting of the housing bubble, the credit freeze, the contraction of consumer demand, or the resulting lost jobs. But they will make a difference.

In this chapter we fit these government insurance success stories into a larger framework of government risk management. Although not always recognized, risk management represents one of the most powerful tools that government has—and one with a long and successful history in the United States. The government has a vital role in managing risk because private markets for risk do not always work optimally on their own. Indeed, this is why programs such as Social Security, Medicare, and federal deposit insurance are among the most successful—and most popular—policies ever adopted in this country.

In the pages that follow, we explain the four basic ways to manage risk: prevention, risk shifting, risk spreading, and loss control. We set out five principles of effective government risk management gleaned from extensive historical study: (1) link responsibility and control, (2) manage moral hazard, (3) pool risk in sound institutions, (4) adopt market conforming approaches to the extent possible, and (5) structure markets to promote safe products. Finally, we describe some promising new government risk management ideas that incorporate these principles.

Risk Management 101

There are four basic ways to manage risk: prevention, risk shifting, risk spreading, and loss control. *Prevention* (or risk reduction) attempts to reduce the frequency and severity of bad things that can happen. Much health and safety regulation falls into this category. *Risk shifting* transfers the responsibility for bad outcomes, often from the person who suffers the initial loss to the person or entity that caused it (or, in some cases, the person or entity best able to absorb and manage the risk). Liability rules fall into this category. *Risk spreading* distributes the costs of particular bad outcomes across a large pool of people. Insurance is the standard loss-spreading institution, and many government programs are forms of insurance. *Loss control* manages or mitigates the consequences after the bad outcome has occurred. Much of the work of fire departments and emergency management agencies, and some of the work of public health and welfare agencies, falls into this category. The sections that follow describe each of these four ways to manage risk, setting the backdrop for our explication of the core principles for government risk management.

Prevention

Prevention, or risk reduction, is a crucial form of risk management. Much government regulation—from speed limits to workplace safety rules—aims directly at loss prevention, and numerous risk reduction strategies are detailed throughout this book. Our main goal in this chapter is to highlight other public policy approaches to risk management and the impact that these other approaches can have on private incentives to reduce risk. For this reason we leave most of the details of prevention to the field specialists in such areas as public health, environmental protection, food and drugs, and occupational safety. Here we focus on ways that risk shifting and risk spreading can promote, or at the very least not undercut, prevention, and on the need to pay attention to loss control.

Risk Shifting

Risk shifting assigns responsibility for a potential future loss to someone other than the person on whom it would initially fall. Risks can be shifted by law, as illustrated by state workers compensation laws, which make employers responsible for many of the financial consequences of occupational injuries. Risks also can be shifted by contract. For example, contracts among owners, builders, and architects specify who will be responsible for which kinds of losses that may occur in the course of designing and building a structure. These contracts operate within a set of background liability rules that leave some losses with the person who directly suffers them and that shift other losses to the person who caused them or who for some other reason is legally responsible. Making these background liability rules is one of the most important risk management activities of government.

Much government risk shifting occurs through liability *creating* rules (such as medical malpractice law), but some very important risk shifting also occurs through liability *limiting* rules (such as limited liability or bankruptcy law). For example, bankruptcy limits people's liability for repaying debts in certain circumstances, providing them with the opportunity to get a fresh start, either as a business or individual. Similarly, there is a federal law that limits consumers' responsibility for unauthorized charges on their credit card accounts. This law facilitated the growth of the credit card market by reducing consumers' fear of credit card fraud. Likewise, corporate law limits the liability of shareholders to the value of their shares, allowing people to invest in businesses without exposing their entire personal net worth. All three of these liability-limiting laws shift risk from borrowers to creditors.

Shifting risk can change people's incentives to prevent loss. Being responsible for a bad outcome increases the incentive to prevent it. Conversely, the ability to shift the risk of that bad outcome to someone else reduces the incentive to prevent it. These incentive effects are an obvious feature of liability-creating rules. But they are an equally important feature of liability-limiting rules. Limiting consumer liability for credit card fraud shifts risk onto credit card companies and, as a result, creates an incentive for those companies to reduce fraud. Credit card companies actively look for unusual transactions using sophisticated computer programs, and they call cardholders for confirmation when a question arises. The limitation on liability provided by bankruptcy law creates an incentive for lenders to monitor borrowers and prevent them from taking on too much debt. And limited liability for shareholders creates an incentive for lenders to examine carefully the operations of corporate borrowers. At the same time, however, those individuals whose liability is limited face a reduced incentive to avoid fraud or excessive risk taking—a problem often referred to as "moral hazard."

Risk shifting can be a flexible, low-cost, and effective government risk management tool, especially in a global economy in which many risks lie beyond the direct reach of the U.S. government. But it is essential that policymakers manage the incentive effects of risk shifting rules in an effective manner. For this reason, several of our risk management principles provide guidance on harnessing these incentives.

Risk Spreading

Risk spreading is a special type of risk shifting, so everything that we have to say about the incentive effects of risk shifting applies to risk spreading as well. Risk spreading differs from other kinds of risk shifting, however, in that the risk of loss shifts to an organization that in turn distributes it broadly, typically by collecting premiums from a large number of people to cover the financial costs of the losses that occur. Insurance is the paradigmatic risk-spreading institution and the primary focus of our analysis here.

There are four main kinds of government insurance: social insurance, financial soundness insurance, catastrophe insurance, and a residual category that we call "market enhancement insurance."

Social insurance protects a population against fundamental risks of life, as a society defines them. Social Security, Medicare, Medicaid, unemployment insurance, workers compensation, and the mandatory minimum amount of automobile insurance are all examples of social insurance in the U.S. Among these, workers compensation and automobile insurance are notable in being provided by private insurance companies in most instances. Health insurance more generally is in the process of being recognized as a form of social insurance in the U.S., and it too is provided largely by private companies.

Financial soundness insurance protects people from the insolvency of important financial institutions such as banks, pension plans, and insurance companies. Typically provided by the government, financial soundness insurance offers customers an additional level of security while generally leaving the provision of the services themselves to the private market. Financial soundness insurance can be *explicit*, meaning that the government protection is created by law and specified in advance, or *implicit*, meaning that people expect that the government will provide the protection even though that protection is not specified by law in advance. The Federal Deposit Insurance Corporation, the Pension Benefit Guaranty Corporation, and the various state insurance guaranty associations provide explicit financial soundness insurance.

Organizations widely believed to be protected by implicit federal government financial soundness insurance include private financial institutions that are "too big to fail" because of the systemic financial risk that could result from their failure. Fannie Mae and Freddie Mac, the federally chartered corporations active in the secondary mortgage market, were widely believed to be protected by implicit financial soundness insurance, a belief that was confirmed when the federal government took them over in 2008. Like many other policy analysts, we strongly prefer explicit insurance to implicit insurance, because implicit insurance generally violates one or more of our risk management principles.

Government *catastrophe insurance* protects people from some of the consequences of catastrophic events that private insurance companies are unable or unwilling to insure. Flood, terrorism, and nuclear accident insurance are the leading examples of federally provided catastrophe insurance in the U.S. Some states also support earthquake and windstorm insurance programs. Like financial soundness insurance, catastrophe insurance can also be explicit or implicit. The National Flood Insurance Program is an example of explicit insurance. After-the-fact disaster relief is an example of implicit insurance.

Market enhancement insurance is our name for the final category of government insurance. As the name suggests, this category includes a variety of insurance programs that facilitate the operation of a market. These programs can support private insurance markets, as illustrated by the residual market mechanisms that exist in many states to facilitate the provision of autoworkers compensation, and property insurance to high-risk individuals or businesses. These programs can also foster other markets, as illustrated by the export-import insurance that the federal government provides to stimulate international trade.

Loss Control

Bad things do happen, sometimes in spite of all that we do to prevent them, at other times precisely because we have not done enough. In either case, being prepared to deal with a loss after it happens can be as important to limiting overall risk—and, in some cases, to maintaining the social fabric—as working to prevent the loss itself. The ongoing effort to recover from Hurricane Katrina is a case in point. Arguably more could have been done to prevent the loss (for example through better maintenance of the levee system), but it was inevitable that a hurricane would eventually hit New Orleans and, therefore, that after-the-fact loss-control efforts would be needed someday. Although a substantial amount had been done to get ready, the loss-control effort stumbled, and the social costs multiplied because the people charged with putting the plans into effect were not sufficiently prepared.[2]

As the Hurricane Katrina case illustrates, loss control is a special kind of prevention directed at managing bad outcomes that do occur. People in the insurance industry discuss losses in terms of frequency and severity and recognize that prevention efforts can be directed at reducing both. Loss control is directed at severity. We distinguish, on the one hand, between severity-reduction efforts such as sprinkler systems, storm shutters, and other efforts to protect vulnerable property and, on the other, efforts to reduce severity by actively managing the overall impact of an adverse event after it occurs, such as emergency response. For us, protection efforts falls into the broader prevention category, while actively managing a loss falls into the narrower loss-control category. In any event, drawing a precise conceptual boundary is much less important than understanding the importance of loss control.

Five Principles of Effective Government Risk Management

We have distilled the relevant research on the topic into five core principles of effective government risk management. The first two principles—*link responsibility with control* and *manage moral hazard*—apply to every government risk management program. The third principle—*pool risk in sound organizations*—applies to risk-spreading programs. The final two principles—*prefer market-conforming approaches* and *structure markets to promote safe products*—reflect a preference for market-based solutions and a prescription for helping them succeed.

We do not claim that these five principles are the beginning and end of government risk management. We do claim, however, that policymakers who ignore these principles—especially the first three—will be disappointed with the results and may even do more harm than good. In what follows, we explain the principles and provide some concrete examples of government risk management programs that successfully apply them.

1. Link Responsibility with Control

We present this principle first to emphasize its importance. Sound risk management requires placing responsibility on people in a position to do something about the risk. Concerned about product safety? Then place responsibility for product injuries on the people who make the products. Concerned about pollution? Then place responsibility for pollution on the polluters. Concerned about borrowers overextending their credit card debt? Then place responsibility on those pushing the credit as well as the borrowers who are "consuming" it.

In many cases, ideas have evolved over time about who is best positioned to control a particular risk. Nineteenth-century accident law, for example, placed most of the responsibility for workplace accidents on workers, not employers, on the grounds that the workers knew about the potential risks of their work and often were the most immediate cause of workplace accidents. Modern workers compensation, by contrast, recognizes that employers have substantial control over the workplace, especially workplace design, and therefore makes employers partly responsible for workplace accidents. Making employers responsible does not eliminate worker responsibility; it simply shifts some of the financial impact from workers to their employers.

As workplace accidents illustrate, control is a relative concept. Rarely does anyone have complete control, at least with respect to a loss that would be significant enough that we would think about getting the government involved. Instead, people have more or less control. Consider product safety. Consumers have some control over whether a product is used properly, while manufacturers have control over how safe the product is if used properly (and, perhaps, how likely it is that the product will be used improperly). Retailers and wholesalers have no direct control over how the product is used or made, but they do have control over what products they offer for sale and, compared to consumers, better information about the products and greater ability to influence manufacturers. For this reason, product liability law assigns responsibility for injuries from defective products not only to manufacturers, but also to retailers and wholesalers. Product liability law also assigns some responsibility to consumers through legal rules that limit liability in cases involving product misuse. As a result, product liability law represents a good attempt to meet the risk management principle of linking responsibility and control, even if it does not always succeed.

2. Manage Moral Hazard

Moral hazard is the term for a threat that arises when responsibility is uncoupled from control. People in control of a loss do not have the same incentive to prevent it when they know that others will be held financially responsible. All forms of insurance and some other forms of risk shifting present this moral hazard problem. For that reason, managing moral hazard is a central concern in the private insurance industry and the primary occupation of many who work in that industry. Here, government should take its cue from the private sector. Moral hazard matters.

There are three well-known and time-tested tools for managing moral hazard: making sure that enough of the loss continues to fall on the insured person to maintain the prevention incentive (for example, insurance deductibles and co-pays); conditioning insurance coverage on a commitment to engage in specific loss-prevention efforts; and insisting that some control over the loss be shifted along with the risk. In shorthand, we refer to these tools as: *leaving some loss with the insured, contracting on care*, and *taking control*. To a very substantial degree, the success and failure of government risk management programs turns on how well it uses these tools.

Federal bank deposit insurance and the "too big to fail" doctrine are both forms of insurance that have the potential to create moral hazard. Deposit insurance explicitly protects depositors from bank failure, and the "too big to fail" concept provides a form of implicit insurance to other bank creditors. These forms of insurance generate moral hazard by reducing the incentives of depositors and other bank creditors to monitor bank solvency and to do business only with the healthiest banks.

Well into the 1970s, the deposit insurance and bank regulation system set up during the New Deal did a good job of managing that moral hazard, using the tools just described. First, the government did not provide full protection. Only the first $100,000 in deposits per person was insured by the FDIC, leaving an incentive to monitor solvency with the very largest depositors (who were likely in a better position than small depositors to do so). Moreover, the application of the "too big to fail" doctrine was sufficiently uncertain that creditors could not be sure that they would be fully protected, especially for credit provided to smaller banks. Second, the government coupled the deposit insurance program with regulations that obligated banks to keep capital reserves and engage in other practices that reduced the risk of failure. This is conceptually similar to the contracting on care that happens in the private insurance context. Finally, the government took some control over prevention from banks—through the bank-supervision process, which authorizes regulators to manage risk by, for example, conducting examinations, prohibiting unsafe practices, and evaluating major transactions.

The definitive history of what happened to banking regulation since the 1970s has yet to be written, but one thing is clear. More and more of what financial institutions did fell outside the reach of the regulators, even as public guarantees—both implicit and explicit—were progressively expanded. Increasing the amount of government insurance while decreasing the government's ability to manage the associated moral hazard had an inevitable outcome: more insured losses. That is exactly what happened in the years leading up the savings and loan failures of the late 1980s and early 1990s, and again—at least in part—in the years leading up to the financial crisis of 2007 to 2009. Whenever public insurance exists, adequate public monitoring (via effective regulation) is absolutely essential to control the inevitable moral hazard.

3. Pool Risks in Sound Organizations

This third risk management principle is so obvious that it almost did not make our list. Yet policymakers violate this principle sufficiently often that we had to include it. The idea is simple to state (but not always simple to implement): organizations that serve as risk pools must have the financial and other capacity needed to handle the risks that they take on. For insurance regulators this principle dominates all others.

Here are several examples of government risk management that violates this principle.

The Pension Benefit Guaranty Corporation

The PBGC insures participants in traditional, defined-benefit pension plans from losing their pension benefits if their employers are unable to pay. Unfortunately, the PBGC does not operate on a financially sound basis. The premiums charged to employers for this protection are too low in relation to the risk. In addition, employers have discretion that allows them to "game the system." For example, there is a variety of rules that allow an employer to report that a pension plan is much better funded than it really is.[3] Although the PBGC is supposed to be entirely funded by employer premiums, and it does not have a formal government guarantee, many people expect that the federal government will bail out the PBGC if it gets into trouble. As a result, even employers operating sound pension plans, and workers in those firms, have little incentive to advocate that the PBGC operate on a financially sound basis.

State-Based Catastrophe Risk Pools

A number of states have created insurance mechanisms to protect their citizens from natural catastrophe risks that are not covered by private insurance policies. The Florida state-based hurricane risk pool, Citizens Property Insurance Corporation (CPIC), is a prominent example. State-based pools are almost always underfunded, for two main reasons. First, most states are too small to fund enough reserves in the early years of a natural-catastrophe risk pool. Second, states often lack the political will to impose adequate risk-based premiums on people who build near a coast, river, or fault line. As a result, there is not enough money on reserve to pay claims when a major disaster hits, particularly during the early years. For example, as researchers from the Wharton School have shown, Florida's CPIC does not charge an adequate premium to property owners living close to the coast and it does not have enough reserves to pay claims from a major hurricane.[4] When the next big hurricane hits Florida, the state's CPIC will have to find more money, most likely from a combination of state government bonds, assessments from private insurers, and possibly even federal support.

Employer-Funded Health Care

U.S. health care policy from at least the 1950s has promoted employment-based health care as the main approach to health insurance for working-age Americans and their children. From a risk-pooling perspective, there are two problems with employment-based health care. First, there is a fundamental mismatch between employees' risk-pooling needs and employers' risk-pooling promise. Employers' promises last only as long as the employment relationship, but employees' health-care risk exposure lasts at least until they reach retirement age and become eligible for Medicare. Second, employers too often are not sound risk-pooling organizations. When an employer goes bankrupt, workers lose both their jobs and their health-care benefits. Moreover, the health-care cost overhang of an aging workforce in a declining industry makes it even harder for companies to survive, as we see in the auto industry today, increasing the likelihood that people will be forced out of the workplace before reaching retirement age. Employment-based health care could operate on a financially sound basis, but perhaps only with some public mechanism for protecting employees from losing their health care when they lose their jobs and for managing the health-care costs of industries with aging workforces.

Exempting Over-the-Counter Credit Default Swaps from Regulation

In the years leading up to the financial crisis of 2007 to 2009, the market for credit default swaps (CDS) grew enormously, providing a form of insurance against losses on credit instruments (from traditional corporate bonds to collateralized debt obligations, or CDOs). One problem with this market is that highly rated financial institutions such as AIG were able to write huge numbers of CDS contracts without putting down any collateral or holding any meaningful reserves. From a risk-pooling perspective, this turned out to be a major mistake. When the downturn came and the riskiness of virtually all credit instruments increased, AIG found itself unable to meet its CDS obligations, and federal policymakers decided they had no choice but to spend more than $100 billion to rescue AIG, or face a financial catastrophe of the first order. Had the government regulated the safety and soundness of AIG's CDS activities, AIG could not have taken on so much risk and would not have needed such an expensive government bailout.

4. Prefer Market-Conforming Approaches to Public Risk Management

This fourth principle reflects the American preference for free enterprise. It suggests, first, that market enhancement should be preferred to market replacement, where possible. Once the government provides a market-replacing risk management service, it can be hard to change that service and harder to eliminate it, even when there is good evidence that the private market is ready to take over some or all of the risk. By contrast, market competition forces companies to adapt their products over time without the need for centralized decision making. For this reason, market-enhancement programs not only are consistent with core American values, they also increase the odds that risk management services can adapt to meet people's needs over time.

Nevertheless, this principle does not mean that the government should never provide a risk management service. Indeed, some of the most visible and successful federal government risk management programs in the U.S. are market-replacement insurance programs: Social Security, unemployment insurance, deposit insurance, and Medicare. In each of these cases, there was and is widespread consensus that the private market could not effectively manage the risks that these government programs took on.

In such cases this market-conforming principle means that the government should preserve the beneficial incentives that the market provides to the greatest extent possible. When a government provides insurance, for example, it should charge a price for that insurance, as it does in each of the programs we just mentioned. Paying a price for government insurance leads people to consider the cost of the insurance, and a risk-based price gives people an incentive to lower their risk, which helps prevent loss.

There are many government insurance programs, even social insurance programs, that are market-enhancement, rather than market-replacement, programs. For example, state governments play a market-enhancing role for workers compensation, automobile insurance, and homeowners' insurance, by creating residual market mechanisms that allow high-risk people and businesses to get insurance.

Whether the government should replace or enhance the market for private health insurance is among the leading public policy issues of the day. Medicare was created as a market-replacement health insurance program, but there was no real market for health insurance for the elderly when Medicare was enacted in 1965. By contrast, we have an active employment-based private health insurance market today. There are legitimate concerns about the high administrative costs of that insurance, however. Moreover, almost no one believes that the private market alone can provide enough affordable insurance for high-risk individuals or for those with very low incomes. In thinking about how best to address the gaps in the private health insurance market, key questions include, first, whether market-enhancement programs will be enough and, second, whether the administrative cost savings offered by a market-replacement program are big enough to justify giving up on the dynamism of the competitive market. Either way, the ultimate policy solution should be market conforming to the extent possible. For example, although Americans with pre-existing conditions should not pay higher (risk-based) premiums, smokers probably should.

The market-conforming principle also applies to prevention and risk shifting. Rules that shift the risk of loss to those with the greatest control over the risk can represent a market-enhancement approach to prevention. Risk shifting gives people an incentive to reduce loss without dictating how they are supposed to do that. For this reason, liability rules, properly created and applied, represent a free-market, bottom-up alternative to command-and-control–style health and safety regulation.

Government-quality regulation often represents another market-conforming approach to public risk management. Ordinary consumers, for example, are not always well positioned to evaluate the safety or quality of many of the goods and services that they use on a daily basis. Medicine, foods subject to undetectable contamination or spoilage, and many financial products are all examples of products that we have to trust in order to consume. Absent quality regulation, markets in these kinds of trust-based goods might not develop at all, or they will be less robust than consumers would want, because consumers don't have enough information to make informed choices. Government quality regulation of goods and services that depend on trust and that cannot be assessed adequately by consumers themselves represents an important mechanism for building and supporting private markets. It has been said, for example, that the modern pharmaceutical market would not exist without the FDA and that the modern mutual fund industry would not have developed without the Investment Company Act of 1940, which set basic standards for mutual funds.

5. Structure Markets to Promote Safe Products

This last principle generalizes from the example of trust-based goods just described. The idea here is to structure markets so that sellers compete in ways that promote safety and other risk management objectives. We do not suggest that the government should pursue safety at any cost, simply that policymakers should be attuned to their ability to structure markets to promote safe products.

In particular, policymakers should be on the watch for, and distinguish between, two kinds of situations: first, when consumers cannot easily tell the difference between the quality of different products and, second, when consumers will not adequately consider the risks posed by different products or will not reliably make reasonable judgments based on those risks. The behavioral economic tools described in chapter 2 of this book provide some promising strategies for identifying these situations.

Both kinds of situations call for quality regulation, but the kind of quality regulation they require is different. If consumers cannot distinguish among the qualities of different products, the government can improve consumer welfare simply by defining and enforcing different grades of quality or mandating the provision of relevant information about the risk. Government grades of beef are one example; energy efficiency ratings are another. If consumers cannot be counted on to adequately consider risks or to make reasonable judgments based on those risks, however, the government may need to do more, for example, by adopting liability rules, taking the riskiest products off the market, or taxing risky products so that the price the consumer pays takes the risks into account. Product liability law is a good example of the liability approach; the Consumer Product Safety Commission is a good example of a government agency that takes unsafe products off the market; and cigarette taxes are a good example of using tax policy to discourage overuse of a risk-creating product.

This last, market-structuring principle applies with special force to risk management products and services. Research and experience show that consumers often have trouble adequately evaluating the quality of insurance and many other risk management products. Insurance advertising provides good evidence of this point. "Like a good neighbor, State Farm is there." "You're in good hands with Allstate." "Nationwide is on your side." These slogans represent efforts to encourage consumers to trust insurance companies, but like most insurance advertising, they do not convey meaningful information about the quality of the products advertised.

This is not a criticism of insurance advertising. Insurance companies know that people need to trust insurance companies or else they won't buy insurance, so the companies do what they can to convey images of trustworthiness and stability. The companies cannot do very much to sell on the basis of quality, because the quality of most insurance products is not observable by ordinary consumers. Most consumers hope never to make a claim and, when they do, they have little or no basis for comparing the quality of the service that they receive. Even health insurance—which many consumers use on a regular basis—is not fundamentally different, because very few people are repeat users of the really big-ticket items. Indeed, one of the best arguments for keeping employment-based health insurance is that employers may be better situated than individuals to evaluate the quality of competing health insurance providers.

What all this means is that there is an important governmental role for regulating the quality of many products, including financial services products and, especially, insurance products. One of the risk management tools that we describe in the next section has the potential to improve the quality of insurance products by providing a way for consumers to compare the quality of the insurance products offered by different companies.

Applications: New Tools for Managing Major Risks

In a short chapter in a short book, we cannot explain all of the permutations of these risk management approaches and principles. Instead, we would like to show how they could be used in practice. This final section briefly describes new tools for managing major risks: import safety, natural catastrophes, health care for the temporarily unemployed, student loans, and systemic financial risk.

Import Safety: Bonded Warranties and Subsidized Testing[5]

Import safety is a hot-button issue. The U.S. imports massive amounts food, medicine, toys, children's clothing, and other products from countries that do not have the same health and safety regulations that we have. Think of the contaminated heparin, the toy trains with lead paint, the melanin-laced candy, and the adulterated pet food that have come from China in recent years. U.S. and European health and safety regulators are working on ways to improve inspections and other procedures in developing countries, but those efforts are not enough by themselves.

One promising policy option could be an import safety warranty program that would supplement these important efforts to improve regulation and testing in developing countries. The program might have four parts. First, importers and sellers of imported products would warrant that the products meet established U.S. safety and health regulations. Second, the importers would back up that warranty by obtaining insurance or posting a bond. Third, consumers would have the option to assign their warranty rights to warranty rights enforcement organizations, preferably with assignment being the default (meaning that the rights would be assigned unless the consumer actively chooses otherwise). Finally, there would be subsidies available for concerned consumers and small retailers who want to send products out for testing, leading to a decentralized testing environment that would supplement government testing and make it harder for importers to evade detection.

To ease enforcement, the warranty would operate in a simple fashion. The warranty would obligate the seller or importer to pay statutory damages based on three factors: the retail price of the product, the seriousness of the risk, and the success of the importer in recalling the unsafe products and providing refunds to consumers. The statute would direct an appropriate government agency to create guidelines that would make these factors easy for a court to apply. The statutory damages would allow the warranty claims of many consumers to be brought in a single enforcement action, led by the warranty rights enforcement organization. Otherwise the importers or sellers could avoid responsibility by making each consumer bring an individual claim and prove their individual damages—an impossible task in too many cases.

The testing subsidy part of the import safety program would allow consumers and small retailers to send product samples for testing at an affordable cost. The federal government would provide coupons that could be used at approved testing labs to obtain a discounted price on approved tests. The testing labs would market their services and provide consumer access to the coupons, most likely on the Internet. Consumers and retailers would pay part of the testing costs themselves, to discourage excessive or unwarranted use of the testing system.

This new idea takes a risk-shifting approach that satisfies our risk management principles. It shifts more of the risk of unsafe products to importers and sellers, who are better positioned than consumers to evaluate risk. (Although sellers and importers do not make or grow the products, they have much better information and greater ability to invest in risk assessment expertise than consumers.) The program requires the consumer to bear some of the cost of the testing, managing the moral hazard that could result if the government bore the entire cost. Because of the insurance or bonding requirement, the program pools risks in financially sound organizations. Finally, it is a market-enhancement program that gives safe products a leg up in the competition for consumer dollars.

Natural Catastrophes: Reinsurance for All-Risk Property Insurance[6]

As Hurricane Katrina reminded us, the private insurance market does not handle natural catastrophe risks on its own. We have a hodgepodge of state and federal government programs that provide coverage for earthquake and flood risks and, in some highly exposed regions, windstorm risk. One promising policy option is replacing this hodgepodge with a federal *reinsurance* program that would allow ordinary insurance companies to sell "all-risk" property insurance policies to protect homeowners and other property holders.

Reinsurance is insurance for insurance companies. Government reinsurance for natural catastrophes would insure insurance companies against natural-catastrophe losses. Private insurance companies would pay risk-based premiums in return for the federal government's commitment to reimburse the insurers for a percentage of the payments that they make for losses arising out of the covered natural-catastrophe risk. The reinsurance approach would improve on the current hodgepodge of government-run direct insurance programs by allowing consumers to buy one insurance policy that covers all of their property risks. This would relieve consumers from battles with their insurance companies about the causes of damage to their homes—wind, which is covered by ordinary homeowners insurance, or flood, which is not—as we saw in the aftermath of

Hurricane Katrina. In addition, it would create a national risk pool for natural catastrophes that would be better able to operate on a financially sound basis than state-based pools. Finally, the reinsurance approach would allow private insurers, if they chose, to experiment with absorbing more natural-catastrophe risk by reducing the amount of the reinsurance that they purchase from the government.

This program also meets our risk management principles. It shifts the risk of insurance coverage gaps from consumers, who are in a poor position to know what coverage they need from whom and what losses are covered by which policy, to insurers and the federal government, which have greater ability to assess the natural-catastrophe risk in any area and control the drafting of contracts in a way that prevents coverage gaps. Because the reinsurance would be priced on the basis of risk, the program would better manage the moral hazard created by natural-catastrophe insurance than the existing government programs (which may encourage people to build homes in disaster-prone areas). A federal reinsurance program is a more sound risk-pooling organization than the state-based windstorm and earthquake pools that it would replace, primarily because of the greater geographic reach of a national pool. Finally, a risk-based reinsurance approach enhances the private insurance market, rather than replacing it with government-run retail insurance.

Unemployment: Insuring the Health-Care Risk

Providing universal access to health care is a bigger problem than we can tackle in this chapter. Nevertheless there is one piece of that problem that could be addressed with a relatively simple risk management tool: adding a new health insurance premium payment feature to unemployment benefits. Existing law (COBRA) gives laid-off workers the right to continue in their employers' health care plan as long as they pay the *full* cost of the plan—*both* the part of the insurance premium that they paid while working and the employers' share (which typically is much larger than the employee's share). With some justification, this has been called a "let them eat cake" approach to unemployment health-care benefits, because laid-off workers are hardly in a position to pay dramatically more for health insurance than they did when they were working. Including a health-care premium payment benefit in unemployment insurance would provide the "bread" that unemployed workers need to preserve health benefits for their families. This new benefit would increase the price of unemployment insurance, but the social-welfare benefits would almost certainly exceed the cost.

Moreover, this modest but important step would meet our risk management principles. First, it would place more of the risk of involuntary unemployment on employers, who have more control over that risk, and less of the risk on workers and their dependents, who have less control. Second, because it would not provide an additional cash benefit to workers, it would probably not represent a major source of moral hazard. Moreover, unemployment insurance already contains moral-hazard control features: unemployment income benefits replace less than all of a worker's income, the benefits are time limited, and recipients are required to actively look for work and accept reasonable offers (though this last requirement is often difficult to enforce). Third, the government has the authority to make sure that the new benefit does not impair the financial soundness of state unemployment insurance pools. Indeed, because of the stress created by the current financial crisis, the state unemployment risk pools already are going to need federal financial assistance. The new health-care benefit could be incorporated in that process. Finally, including this premium payment benefit in unemployment insurance would enhance the market for private health insurance by keeping more people more consistently in the health-care risk-spreading pool, and it would enhance the market for health-care services by allowing more people to maintain their existing relationships with doctors and other health-care providers. In this regard the premium payment benefit would be superior to the current proposal to provide Medicaid benefits to the unemployed, because many health-care providers do not accept patients who are on Medicaid.

Unsafe Financial Products: The Insurance Transparency Project

Many insurance products differ from other financial products in one fundamental respect: the consumer only has access to insurance money when something bad happens and the insurance company has tremendous discretion over the claims process. For example, with auto insurance, the consumer can only file a claim after an accident; with homeowners insurance, only after a fire, flood, or other unwanted event. This means that the quality of traditional insurance products consists not only in the explicit terms of the insurance contract, but also in the insurance company's approach to paying claims. With banks and mutual funds, by contrast, consumers don't need to worry about the companies' approach to paying claims. With a bank account or mutual fund consumers can take out their money whenever they want.

Today it is impossible for a consumer to reliably evaluate an insurance company's approach to paying claims. Consumers Union conducts some consumer satisfaction surveys and publishes the results in *Consumer Reports* magazine, but we cannot assess the validity of those surveys by comparing them to objective evaluations of companies' claims-paying history, because there are no such evaluations. Of course, people can talk to their friends and neighbors, and state insurance departments maintain records of consumers' complaints. But none of these information sources provide any basis to distinguish among insurance products and companies in any way that is even remotely comparable to what is possible for cars and appliances, for example.

Given advances in information technology, it would be possible for a trusted third party to obtain claims information in electronic form from insurance companies that would allow them to be rated on a scale similar to the credit scores that financial service companies use to rate consumers.[7] This could be done by the Treasury Department, by a new federal insurance regulator, or even by the National Association of Insurance Commissioners, the coordinating body for the existing state-based insurance regulatory system.

This new idea satisfies our risk management principles. Such a system would place responsibility for good claims behavior on the entities in control of that behavior—insurance companies. It would manage the moral hazard that results when insurance companies are able to sell products that promise to pay claims but are then free to delay or shirk when it comes time to pay. It would encourage consumers to buy insurance from companies with a good track record, thereby pooling more risk in sound organizations. It would enhance the insurance market. And it would structure that market to help good companies with good insurance products win the competition for consumers' insurance dollars.

Income-Contingent Student Loans[8]

Economists have long recognized the need for a government role in student lending—because the student loan market does not work like the ordinary credit market. When businesses borrow to buy new machines or individuals borrow to buy a house or car, they can use the machine, the house, or the car as collateral. But when a student borrows for college, there's no tangible asset to collateralize. If the student does not repay the loan, there is nothing for the creditor to seize. Fortunately, we gave up debtors' prisons long ago.

The economist Milton Friedman identified this problem as early as 1955, noting that a working market for student loans hardly existed at that time. A decade later federal policymakers began guaranteeing student loans to help build this market. Although private lending to students rose sharply as a result, the system remains far from perfect. Students who borrow to cover tuition and living expenses put themselves at risk. Awash in debt after graduating, they not only face financial pressure to avoid worthwhile but low-paying jobs (teaching, for example), but they also have to hope for no delays in finding a job, and no significant interruptions once their careers have commenced. Their debt-service payments will remain fixed, whether they have a high-paying job or not.

Fortunately, we could ease this burden by changing the way we finance higher education. Instead of guaranteeing lenders against bad loans (as we currently do), we could protect students from losses on their educational investments. Specifically, we could ensure that every single American could pay for college or graduate school (or job training) on the basis of a federal income-contingent loan. The loan could extend up to thirty years (like a mortgage) and would reduce or eliminate annual payments if the recipient's household income fell below a predetermined trigger.

In addition to expanding access to higher education, this loan program would also reduce costs. Under the current approach, the federal government guarantees roughly three-quarters of all loans for postsecondary education. Private lenders benefit when the loans are repaid, and the federal government is stuck with the losses when students default. The federal government also pays for private collection services, which are often provided by the very lenders whose "losses" were covered by federal guarantees in the first place. Under the new program, collection would be undertaken by the IRS, through regular tax withholding. Repayment would thus occur almost automatically, reducing delinquency rates and allowing for a lower interest rate on the loans.

This idea satisfies our risk management principles far better than the current approach, which decouples responsibility from control. Under the existing system, private lenders have a strong incentive to make loans, even to less-than-creditworthy borrowers, since the federal government assumes all of the risk through its guarantees. In fact, the appeal of private gains without the risk of loss has been so great that many lenders cut corners (ethical and perhaps even legal) in a drive for market share. Under the new program, the federal government would assume both the risk and the responsibility for making collections. Most important of all, students would see their risk drop (since they would not have to repay their loans if their income faltered), and this would almost inevitably expand participation in higher education—a big benefit both for the students themselves and for American society as a whole.

Some might say that the program violates our fourth principle (prefer market-conforming approaches), since the new government program would displace private lenders. But in fact the existing system is in no real sense private, since the federal government already bears all of the risk. The new approach would strengthen incentives and put the federal guarantee where it belongs—behind students, rather than behind the banks that lend to them.

Managing Systemic Risk in the Financial System[9]

In 2008, terms such as *systemic risk* and *too big to fail* took on new meaning in the face of a powerful financial storm. Financial contagion had been a recurring problem for much of American history, with major crises striking just about every fifteen to twenty years from 1792 to 1933. After that, however, the nation enjoyed more than fifty years of relative financial stability following the introduction of federal deposit insurance and other New Deal financial reforms. In time, many Americans probably came to take this favorable state of affairs for granted. The S&L debacle of the mid- to late 1980s temporarily disrupted the calm, but even so it was hardly a major crisis by historical standards. By contrast, the financial crisis of 2007 to 2009 has threatened many of the central pillars of the American financial system, from investment banking and insurance companies to money market funds and the commercial-paper market.

In addressing the crisis, federal officials have attempted to calm markets and rescue ailing institutions by spreading financial resources, especially in the form of guarantees, in virtually every direction—more than $10 trillion in potential commitments by the end of 2008, according to the Congressional Budget Office. Large-scale risk absorption by the federal government quickly became the strategy of choice, though unfortunately with few of the necessary safeguards against moral hazard. Perhaps there was no other choice, given the pace and magnitude of the crisis. Looking forward, however, it is imperative that policymakers take control of the situation, reducing or eliminating the dangerous incentives that they have created along the way.

Of particular concern are the implicit federal guarantees that now swaddle every financial institution that appears "too big to fail." Federal rescues of leading financial firms—from Bear Stearns, Fannie Mae, and Freddie Mac to AIG and Citigroup—have sent a clear signal that such large and strategic firms cannot be allowed to collapse, since the systemic consequences of failure could prove catastrophic, setting off an avalanche of losses. The willingness of federal officials to allow Lehman Brothers to declare bankruptcy under Chapter 11—and the severe market turmoil that followed—made this the exception that proved the rule. The main downside of this too-big-to-fail strategy is moral hazard, since creditors, counterparties, and shareholders of major financial firms will inevitably let down their guard, hopeful that the federal government will come to the rescue, particularly in cases of systemic turmoil. In the absence of careful management, such moral hazard will almost certainly invite excessive risk taking and greater financial losses in the future.

One solution would be to identify and regulate—and potentially even insure—"systemically significant" financial institutions in normal times, rather than simply waiting for a crisis to strike. At the present time, federal officials wait until a financial firm is on the verge of failure to decide if it is systemically significant—that is, if its failure would be likely to provoke broader financial turmoil and cascading losses. By that time, however, the situation is already critical. Instead, officials should decide which institutions are systemically significant on an ongoing basis (that is, in normal times), and institutions found to be "systemically significant" should be regulated more stringently than others to guard against moral hazard and make failure less likely.

In particular, systemically significant institutions should face stricter leverage and liquidity ratios, reducing the likelihood that they would get into trouble in the first place or contribute to a downward spiral by having to dump already falling assets in a downturn. Systemically significant institutions might also be required to buy federal capital insurance, which would collect premiums in normal times and offer prespecified capital infusions to *all* systemically significant institutions (not just ailing ones) in times of crisis. In this way, the current open-ended implicit guarantees would be made explicit—and explicitly limited. Finally, systemically significant institutions that reach insolvency in any case (despite the tougher regulation and federal capital insurance) should be put through an FDIC-style receivership process, rather than being allowed to enter Chapter 11 bankruptcy, which is ill-suited to handle the failure of major financial institutions. This would ensure that no firm can ever grow too big to fail, further reducing the moral hazard stemming from the recent federal rescues.

An important advantage of the proposed system is that it would discourage financial institutions from becoming systemically significant in the first place. This is just the opposite of the situation that obtains now, in which financial firms have good reason to become too big to fail, so as to garner a free implicit guarantee from the federal government. This troubling incentive can be corrected by being clear about the systemic significance of financial institutions and regulating (and potentially insuring) them in normal times, rather than waiting to act until a crisis arises. Such an approach would put a premium on prevention (as opposed to just crisis management) and importantly would meet all of our principles, including in particular our second principle regarding the need to manage moral hazard.

Conclusion

Policymakers from across the political spectrum agree that governments are, inevitably, in the risk management business. As the current financial crisis demonstrates, government is the risk manager of last resort. Properly designed public risk management programs are among the most powerful government tools and the most popular and successful government programs.

We have set out a set of simple but important principles of effective government risk management drawn from extensive historical study. When managing risk, the government should link responsibility and control, manage moral hazard, pool risk in sound organizations, adopt market-conforming approaches to the greatest extent possible, and structure markets to promote safe products.

To illustrate how these principles work in practice, and also to provide some new ideas for policymakers to consider, we have sketched out six new risk management programs: bonded import safety warranties, natural catastrophe reinsurance, health-care continuation benefits for the unemployed, an insurance transparency project, income-contingent student loans, and systemic risk management for the financial system. Not all of these programs are ready for immediate adoption, but together they suggest the possibility of a new era in government risk management.

Notes

1 This chapter draws conceptually from David Moss, *When All Else Fails: Government as the Ultimate Risk Manager* (Cambridge: Harvard University Press, 2002); Tom Baker, *Insurance Law and Policy*, 2nd ed. (New York: Aspen Publishing, 2008); and Tom Baker, *On the Genealogy of Moral Hazard, Texas Law Review* 72 (1997): 237.

2 *See* the U.S. Government Accountability Office's "Catastrophic Disasters: Enhanced Leadership, Capabilities, and Accountability Controls Will Improve the Effectiveness of the Nation's Preparedness, Response, and Recovery System" (GAO-06-618, 2006, at 99–100). This report to congressional committees made recommendations in the wake of Hurricane Katrina for executive action regarding the nation's preparedness, and its response and recovery system. *See also*: "A Failure of Initiative: The Final Report of the Select Bipartisan Committee to Investigate the Preparation for and Response to Hurricane Katrina," U.S. House of Representatives 163 (2006): http://katrina. house.gov/full_katrina_report.htm (last visited February 8, 2009).

3 *See* Jeffrey R. Brown, "Guaranteed Trouble: The Economic Effects of the Pension Benefit Guaranty Corporation," *Journal of Economic Perspectives* 22, no. 1 (Winter 2008): 177–98. The PBGC also violates the principle of managing moral hazard by charging the same premiums to employers operating a conservatively funded pension plan and those operating a poorly funded plan.

4 *See* Howard C. Kunreuther and Erwann O. Michel-Kerjan, *At War with the Weather* (Cambridge, MA: MIT Press, 2009).

5 This idea will be developed further in a chapter by Tom Baker in Cary Coglianese, Adam Finkel, and David Zaring, eds., *Import Safety: Regulatory Governance in the Global Economy* (forthcoming 2010).

6 *See* David Moss, "Courting Disaster: The Transformation of Federal Disaster Policy Since 1803," in Kenneth A. Froot, ed., *The Financing of Catastrophe Risk* (Chicago: University of Chicago Press, 1999).

7 This excellent idea is not ours. We borrowed it, and the label, from Dean Starkman, the creator of the Insurance Transparency Project blog, which tracked the insurance aftermath of Hurricane Katrina.

8 Adapted from David Moss, "Leave No Risk Behind," On My Mind, *Forbes*, July 23, 2007. Available at http://www.forbes.com/forbes/2007/0723/036.html.

9 *See* David Moss, "An Ounce of Prevention: The Power of Public Risk Management in Stabilizing the Financial System" (HBS Working Paper 09-087, January 2009).

CHAPTER 5

Toward a Culture of Persistent Regulatory Experimentation and Evaluation[1]

Michael Greenstone

> *The country needs and, unless I mistake its temper, the country demands bold, persistent experimentation. It is common sense to take a method and try it: If it fails, admit it frankly and try another. But above all, try something.*

—Franklin Delano Roosevelt, Address at Oglethorpe University, May 22, 1932

> *The question we ask today is not whether our government is too big or too small, but whether it works—whether it helps families find jobs at a decent wage, care they can afford, a retirement that is dignified. Where the answer is yes, we intend to move forward. Where the answer is no, programs will end.*

—Barack Obama, Inaugural Address, January 20, 2009

American government, at every level, regulates a dizzyingly broad swath of social and economic life. Regulatory policy determines the drugs we can buy, the pollutants in the air we breathe, the quality of the water we drink, the speed at which we can drive, the materials we use to construct our homes, the cars we buy, the rules that govern our employment contracts, the loans we can take out, the investments we make, and so much more. In making decisions about regulations, public officials must choose which areas of our lives merit government rules, as well as how stringent those rules should be. The essence of regulation is that it requires the regulated to take actions that they would not otherwise take, actions that often increase their costs, reduce their utility, or in some other way harm them. When faced with this incredible array of complex and often uncertain trade-offs, what is a well-intentioned government to do?

The current system for making these choices is broken. It is largely based on faith, rather than evidence. The efficacy of many regulations is never assessed. Many others are only evaluated *before* they are implemented—the point when we know the least about them. The result is that our regulatory system all too frequently takes shots in the dark and we all too infrequently fail to find out if we have hit anything—or even worse, we only find out when things have gone horribly wrong.

But it doesn't have to be this way. We already have an example of scientifically based regulation in our approach to determining which foods and drugs are safe via the Food and Drug Administration (FDA). The FDA-led double-blind testing of pharmaceutical drugs has led to a revolution in medicine, and drugs are now safer than they have ever been before. The basis of the FDA's system is the recognition that it is impossible to know whether a drug is beneficial in advance of its use.

Why should we choose the regulations that govern our society less carefully than the foods we eat and drugs we ingest?

I. A New Era in Regulatory Reform

This essay is a call to move toward a culture of persistent regulatory experimentation and evaluation. Our goal should be to rigorously evaluate every regulation in order to expand upon the ones that work and weed out the ones that fail to improve our well-being (or worse, harm it). At the heart of such reform is the recognition that we cannot know a regulation's benefits and costs until it has been tested. The rewards for such testing are better regulations, which can improve our lives, our children's lives, and those of our children's children.

In many respects, a culture of regulatory experimentation and evaluation is the logical next phase of the American regulatory project. We have now followed two paths and found both to be lacking. The first push for regulation came out of the New Deal and the Great Society and simply emphasized doing something to correct abuses and other social ills. In many instances, the mere act of trying to do something seemed to be the goal, and evaluation and follow-up were not emphasized.

Eventually, this age of regulation was supplanted by a second era, which emphasized the failures of the first. This second phase, which was broadly associated with the Reagan years, introduced a faith in the free market to produce desired societal outcomes.

A culture of persistent regulatory experimentation and evaluation would build upon both of these great ages and propel us into a third era of regulatory reform. This culture would meld together the wish to establish national policies that enhance the well-being of our citizens and the insistence that this be done credibly and cost-effectively, given fiscal constraints. The tools of experimentation necessary to achieve this goal are available and are already being used in a variety of other contexts. Used widely, they will lead us to a new era of effective regulatory policy.

II. Credible Cost-Benefit Analysis

The only humane approach to regulation is to require that every rule and policy be subject to a credible cost-benefit analysis. The most important task in the reforming of our system of regulation is to determine which regulations work and which do not. Cost-benefit analysis provides a rational, quantitative method for determining how well individual regulations are working. All regulations have expected benefits (for example, lives saved, illnesses prevented) and expected costs (investments required to scrub smokestacks, expenditures on monitoring pollution emissions). Government's task is to identify and implement regulations whose benefits exceed their costs; cost-benefit analysis is the tool that makes this possible.

Cost-benefit analysis requires that all of the disparate costs and benefits of a particular regulation be converted to a common unit, nearly always money. By converting all costs and benefits to the same unit, government can avoid irrational combinations of policies that fail to maximize our well-being. The costs and benefits for one person under one policy are treated no differently than the costs and benefits for another person under another policy.

The current regulatory problem is not a lack of cost-benefit analysis.[2] Some form of cost-benefit analysis already underlies most regulatory decisions. Rather, the problem is the poor quality of the evidence underlying many applications. Indeed, critics of cost-benefit analysis have argued that it can be twisted to produce desired results. One major reason for these criticisms is that most cost-benefit analyses are not performed in a credible manner.

The single greatest problem with the current system is that most regulations are subject to a cost-benefit analysis only in advance of their implementation. This is the point when the least is known and any analysis must rest on many unverifiable and potentially controversial assumptions. There is a place for such prospective analyses in providing a first pass at assessing regulations. Even if regulators are well intentioned, however, the problem remains that it is not possible to know the causal impact of a policy in advance.

How can regulators determine the true effect of policies? The first step is to admit that it is generally impossible to assess regulations prospectively. Under the current system, regulations are typically evaluated *before* they are implemented and rarely examined again once they have been put in place. Since the regulations have not yet been enforced, these prospective evaluations involve an unhealthy dose of blind faith. Whatever its origins, it is an approach to choosing effective regulations that involves the government tying at least one hand behind its back.

Indeed, it is nearly impossible to imagine this approach being used in other contexts where people's lives are on the line. For example, I am confident that there would be a deafening uproar of protest if the FDA announced that it would approve drugs without testing them in advance. Yet, this is largely what we do with regulations that affect our health and well-being.

The second step is to adopt a culture of regulatory experimentation and evaluation. I will outline below a specific plan to introduce such a system. However, at its core, this reform is simple. It involves rigorously testing all regulations and then expanding upon the regulations that work and dropping the ones that do not.

The FDA's drug approval process is a good example of a system of experimentation and evaluation. Each new drug is subjected to four phases of testing, slowly ramping up from small randomized trials of fifteen to thirty people to widespread use. After clinical trials are completed, all of the evaluations are reviewed by the Center for Drug Evaluation and Research (CDER). The CDER employs doctors, pharmacologists, chemists, statisticians, and other relevant professionals. In the review process, these professionals scrutinize each aspect of the new drug's application. If the burden of evidence has been met that the drug is safe and effective, it can be distributed to the public. Such a system could easily be adapted for regulation.

III. The Case for Credible Estimates of Costs and Benefits

A. Too Much Money Spent Saving Too Few Lives

We should experiment more in regulation, because the body of evidence regarding the costs and benefits of regulation is sparse. The paucity of evidence is partly explained by the impossibility of knowing beforehand whether a regulation will pass a cost-benefit test. Proponents of a new regulation inevitably argue that its benefits are substantial, while opponents inevitably argue that the costs are too high. The difficulty is that the evidence needed to assess such claims is almost always unavailable.

The result is that all too often regulatory decisions are based on rhetoric. This means that we almost surely devote too many resources to regulations that have small net benefits and not enough to regulations with big net benefits.

For example, there is a wide range of cost-effectiveness even under already established rules. One study (Morrall 2003) collected estimates of the cost per statistical life saved from agency Regulatory Impact Analyses (RIAs), and found significant variation in the efficiency of regulations. Restrictions that lighters be manufactured so that they are childproof saves lives for about $100,000 per life, as do OSHA's respiratory protection rules. On the other hand, so few lives are saved relative to the cost of the EPA's Solid Waste Disposal Facility Criteria that every statistical life saved costs an estimated $100 billion.

If these numbers are taken literally, they imply that the amount of money required to save *one life* with the Solid Waste Disposal regulation would save *one million lives* with the respiratory protection rules. Although the estimates in the Morrall study are unlikely to be credible, since they are derived from prospective RIAs, the point is that our current regulatory regime causes us to pass up opportunities to save lives without incurring any extra costs. This is not a humane approach to regulation.

Another example of regulatory decision making based on poor evidence is the debate that surrounded the catalytic converter (McCarthy 2007). In the 1970s, automobiles were the target of a wide variety of new pollution standards in the United States. In particularly, new fuel emissions standards meant that the installation of catalytic converters was required on automobiles for the first time. These converters use chemical reactions to reduce the amounts of pollutants released in automobile exhaust. The car industry and its interest groups lobbied strongly against these regulations, leading the public to believe that requiring converters would lead to all sorts of dire consequences. At the time, it was common to claim that the direct cost of the converters would be as much as $300 per car, when it in fact turned out to be closer to $165 per car. Similarly, the Big Three automakers said that fuel economy would fall by as much as 20 percent after installing converters and switching to unleaded gasoline. However, the first model of car to have the required converter had a 13.5 percent *higher* fuel economy, on average, than the previous model. Finally, it was thought that catalytic converters would have to be replaced every 25,000 miles, when in fact they still ran at a reasonable level of efficiency after even 50,000 miles. Estimates before regulations are actually undertaken can be distorted by interested parties—or just plain wrong.

These examples illustrate that the inefficiencies in the current regulatory system mean that we are passing up opportunities to save lives and money. This is not a humane situation, yet it arises over and over again in our broken regulatory system. The introduction of a culture of experimentation into our regulatory system is the only humane solution.

B. The Evaluation Problem

The development of reliable estimates of the costs and benefits of regulations begins with the specification of a causal hypothesis or hypotheses. The key features of a causal hypothesis are that it contains a manipulable treatment that can be applied to a subject and an outcome that may or may not respond to the treatment. For example, we may hypothesize that a regulation aiming to reduce air pollution in a city will reduce mortality rates among residents. For a causal hypothesis to have any practical relevance, we must be able to subject it to a meaningful test. Such a test requires that all other determinants of the outcome be held constant so that the effect of the treatment can be isolated.

Ideally it would be feasible to observe simultaneously the same subjects in two different states: one in which the regulation is applied, and one in which it is not. This would guarantee that all other factors are held constant. Of course, it is impossible to observe both states simultaneously. For example, the regulation to reduce air pollution cannot simultaneously be administered to *and* withheld from the same city. This impossibility is labeled the *fundamental problem of causal inference.*

This problem is relevant for cost-benefit analysis in at least two different ways. First, many regulations are implemented for an entire population, which makes it impossible to develop a valid counterfactual case for what would have happened in the absence of a regulation's implementation. In the absence of a counterfactual, it is impossible to know the policy's causal impacts.

The second problem occurs when a regulation is applied to some people or places and not to others, while these two differ in important ways. This is called *selection bias* and it occurs when there is a control group, but the regulated or treatment group differs from the control group. For example, suppose we want to evaluate the effects of a job-training program. One way to structure the analysis would be to compare people who sign up for the program with others who are similar, according to observable characteristics. The problem is that the people who sign up may differ from those who do not in an unobserved way. The result is that a comparison of the two sets of people will confound the impact of the program with these pre-existing differences. Indeed, Ashenfelter (1978) and Ashenfelter and Card (1985) demonstrate that this is a real problem in the context of a job-training program.

The point is that credible cost-benefit analysis requires the identification of a solution to the fundamental problem of causal inference.

C. Experiments and Quasi Experiments Solve the Evaluation Problem

The gold standard for estimating the causal impact of a regulation is the *randomized trial*. This approach starts with a population of people, businesses, or places that could potentially be subject to the regulation. Among this population, some are randomly assigned to the *treatment group* and the regulation is applied to them. The others are randomly assigned to the *control group* and receive no regulation. Because of this random assignment, the treatment and control groups should be statistically identical in all dimensions except exposure to the regulation; thus, any differences in outcomes can be ascribed to the regulation. Put another way, with a randomized experiment, it is valid to assume that a comparison of outcomes among the treatment and control groups yields an estimate of the causal effect of the regulation.

The use of randomized experiments outside medicine is growing rapidly, so there is a precedent for the application of this strategy to testing government regulations. Randomized trials have been used to assess the impacts of job-training programs, policies to reduce student-teacher ratios in elementary schools, the impacts of indoor air pollution on human health in developing countries, and even the impacts of maternal smoking on infant health (some mothers in the trial were given additional encouragement to quit smoking). It is becoming evident that this approach can be applied successfully in a wider variety of settings than has previously been thought.

It is worth noting that some consider randomized experiments unethical, because they relegate a significant number of people to the control group when there are nonexperimental reasons to believe that the treatment or regulation will prove beneficial. In many regulatory contexts, however, some people or places will not receive the treatment because of cost or budgetary concerns. In this case, I argue that the most ethical assignment rule is to assign the regulations randomly, because this approach is transparent and free of political considerations. Further, in most cases a regulation's benefits are truly unknown in advance and would remain so without a credible evaluation. Thus, the experiences of the few in the control and treatment groups can be used to benefit society as a whole.

The second potentially credible form of evaluation is the *quasi experiment.* In a quasi experiment, the causal effect is also given by the difference in outcomes between a treatment group and a control group. However, in quasi experiments the assignment of individual subjects to the treatment or control group is determined by nature, politics, an accident, or some other factor. Despite the nonrandom assignment of treatment status, it may still be possible to draw valid inferences from the differences in outcomes between the treatment and control groups. The validity of the inference rests on the assumption that assignment to the treatment and control groups is not related to other determinants of the outcomes.

An example of a quasi experiment comes from a recent paper that aims to estimate the impact of Superfund sponsored cleanups of hazardous waste sites on nearby property values (Greenstone and Gallagher 2008). The difficulty for causal inference is to understand what would have happened to property values in the absence of the cleanup.

The paper's quasi-experimental solution is based on knowledge of the selection rule that the Environmental Protection Agency (EPA) used to develop the first set of sites to be cleaned up after Superfund became law in 1980. The EPA was only allocated enough money to conduct four hundred cleanups. After cutting the list of candidate sites from 15,000 to 690, the EPA invented and implemented the Hazardous Ranking System (HRS) that assigned each site a score from 0 to 100 based on the risk it posed, with 100 being the most dangerous. The four hundred sites with the highest HRS scores (those exceeding 28.5) were placed on the initial list of sites eligible for Superfund remedial cleanups. The paper then compares the evolution of housing market outcomes between 1980 and 2000 in areas near sites that had initial HRS scores above and below the 28.5 threshold. It also compares sites that nearly missed eligibility with sites that just qualified for the cleanups.

Both randomized trial experiments and quasi experiments can be used to solve the fundamental problem of causal inference. The missing step is their implementation.

IV. Regulatory Reform in Four Simple Steps

The key to reforming the regulatory system is to instill a culture of experimentation and evaluation. This can be established in four simple steps.

A. Experiment, Experiment, Experiment!

1. Structure Regulations so that Evaluations are Feasible

The first step toward a culture of regulatory experimentation and evaluation is to write the statutes governing regulatory programs so that the regulations are implemented in ways that they lend themselves to experimental or quasi experimental evaluation. This can be achieved in at least two different ways.

If possible, regulations should be launched on a small scale before being applied to a large population. This approach has several advantages. First, it allow for experimentation. Small-scale implementation leaves the space to create randomly assigned treatment and control groups. Second, it allows different forms of the regulation to be tested. Third, it limits the damage if the regulation is found to fail a cost-benefit test.

The second way to experiment is to allow states to implement different regulations. In particular, the American federal system provides an opportunity to implement regulations on a small scale before expanding them to a larger scale. States can try out regulations (for example, Massachusetts's health care program or California's history of stringent environmental regulations) on a small scale, and if they succeed, it is frequently possible to scale them up to the federal level. Supreme Court Justice Louis Brandeis is often quoted as saying that states are the laboratories of democracy. Certainly states can become quite literally laboratories for regulatory experiments.

In cases where a true randomized experiment is infeasible, it is still possible to structure regulations that are amenable to evaluation. This can be done by using quasi-experimental assignment techniques. One technique that has proven quite effective is to assign the treatment to places or people based on an objective score or criterion. Indeed, this is the basis for the quasi experiment used to evaluate the impact of Superfund cleanups of hazardous waste sites that I have described above.

The key point, though, is that new regulations should be implemented so that evaluations of their impacts are possible. If this easy step is not taken, then it will never be possible to know any regulation's true costs and benefits.

2. Fund Evaluations, Collect Data, and Publicly Release the Data

Clearly, it is not sufficient merely to devise regulations in such a way that they are intrinsically testable; we have to fund the evaluations of new regulations also. An easy way to achieve this would be for the president to sign an executive order mandating that all new regulations must include provisions for collecting data that allow for evaluations of their effectiveness.

The funds devoted to such research should be used for evaluations by independent research groups (for example, academics or private companies) and should adhere to the highest standards in research design and data analysis. Although high-quality evaluations can be costly, the costs usually pale in comparison to the costs imposed by regulations that have small benefits.

Further, the public's confidence in government can be increased by releasing de-identified data generated in these evaluations on government Web sites.[3] This will enhance the credibility of the evaluations by making them transparent. If the official evaluators reach conclusions that the data contradict, the public will be able to highlight this. Indeed, the potential for replication and exposing mistakes will serve as an incentive for those performing the analyses to get it correct the first time.

B. Create a Regulatory Review Board

Washington is filled with reports and evaluations. Indeed, many agencies already provide evaluations of the regulations that they oversee and administer. However, history is not kind to organizations that only engage in self-evaluation. It is very difficult for people and organizations to conclude that despite their best efforts their policies or programs are ineffective. Moreover, those who are deeply involved in the implementation of a particular regulation are likely to see the benefits of such a project far more clearly than the costs.

A solution to this problem is to create an independent regulatory review board that has the authority to assess the effectiveness of regulations. The board would review all available studies and could fund additional studies. They would then use the available evidence to assess whether a regulation passes a cost-benefit analysis.

Based on these assessments, this board must have the power to repeal regulations that are deemed ineffective. This may sound radical, but similar powers are granted to bureaucracies in other contexts. For example, the FDA has the right to prevent drugs from being sold on the open market. Ideally, this power to repeal a regulation would be explicit in the wording of the regulation itself. Of course, Congress and the president would have the right to overrule such a review board, but the default procedure should to permit the review board's rulings stand.

Furthermore, the regulatory review board should consist of well-respected professionals and academics who have the technical ability to review evaluations critically *and* do not have a stake in whether a regulation remains on the books. The appointment of top-notch, impartial people is crucial because it will help to insulate the regulatory review board from claims of bias. The key is to make the board nonideological and technocratic.

While a regulatory review board may seem like a big departure from current policies, there are plenty of precedents for providing review boards with power. The FDA is an obvious example. Additionally, funding organizations such as the National Institutes of Health (NIH) and the National Science Foundation (NSF) use independent review boards to determine which grant proposals should be funded. These boards consist of as few as three and as many as thirty members. Typically at least one member of the board is a full-time employee of the organization and the remaining members are drawn from the academic community. A few members of the board are selected to read each proposal and present it to the board with a rating for its scientific merit. This sort of board structure would also work well in regulation. After an evaluation of a regulation has been conducted, a board could convene that would study the evaluation and reach a conclusion.

It is noteworthy that there already exists a part of the executive branch that aims to undertake some of the functions that I have outlined for a regulatory review board. The Office of Information and Regulatory Affairs (OIRA) is a subdivision of the Office of Management and Budget (OMB) in the White House. The executive order that determines OIRA's role specifically calls for centralized review and cost-benefit analysis of all regulations, as advocated here.

However, OIRA lacks a few of the key elements discussed above. First, there is no requirement that cost-benefit analyses be credible in the ways that

I have proposed. Second, most reviews of regulations are prospective instead of retrospective. Without actual evidence for what regulations have done, rather than theoretical estimates of what they might do, the resulting estimates of costs and benefits are unlikely to be credible. Again, it is preposterous to imagine the FDA using this type of evaluation technique. Third, OIRA can review regulations directly, but it is not an independent review board. It is headed by political appointees and is subject to the constraints that such organizations have.

The idea of the regulatory review board is to take some of the functions of OIRA and transfer them to an independent, bipartisan commission created for this purpose. This commission would identify opportunities for evaluating regulation, find and assign evaluators to these cases, and convene independent review boards to consider evaluations and pass final judgment on them. As much as possible, these functions should be removed from political control and placed in independent hands.

C. Automatic Sunset and Expansion Provisions

The third step in reforming our regulatory system is to require that all regulations contain rules specifying the date by which the regulatory review board has to assess their costs and benefits. If the regulatory review board fails to meet one of these deadlines, then the regulation should be repealed by default. The purpose of this sunset provision is to ensure that all regulations are evaluated carefully and do not stay on the books just because they have been on the books in the past.

Of at least equal importance is that regulations that are shown to pass a cost-benefit test should become part of our regulatory portfolio and potentially expanded. Indeed, every regulation should detail how it may be expanded if it is shown to be effective. For example, if a given regulation was originally enacted only in a small-scale trial form, its scope should be widened to include all relevant actors. Thus, a judgment by the regulatory review board that a regulation is effective should automatically lead to its expansion to any parts of the economy where it does not yet apply.

Of course, there will be situations in which political goals will be more important. In these cases, lawmakers have the power to exempt a regulation from this process. However, the purpose of the automatic sunset and expansion provisions is to ensure that the default procedure should be for credible evidence on regulations' effectiveness to translate into action.

D. Develop and Apply a Code of Ethics

People frequently have a visceral reaction against experiments that involve humans, even though the FDA and other organizations use them out of necessity. At least some of this reaction is due to such drastic breaches of medical ethics as the horrific and immoral Tuskegee syphilis and Nazi medical experiments. These experiments were unethical because they failed to treat people with a disease and exposed people to life-threatening and unnecessary interventions, respectively.

By contrast, experimentation with regulation is concerned with testing solutions to problems, not with observing the problems themselves. Much like FDA testing of new medicines, it is safer and more humane to test new regulations on small groups of people before extending their scope.

Nevertheless, an important component of a culture of persistent regulatory experimentation and evaluation involves the creation of a code of research ethics that ensures the safety of humans and the appointment of a board to ensure that regulatory experiments are ethical. The Nuremberg Code was adopted in medicine after the Nazi medical experiments and it may provide a good starting point for a code of ethics that governs regulatory experimentation. One model for the development of boards to prevent ethical violations comes from university institutional review boards, which ensure that experiments by their faculty are conducted in an ethical manner.

V. Getting There from Here

The implementation of the call for reform of the regulatory system that I have detailed here would require many changes to the current system. Several of these changes would require the passage of new legislation. However, it is possible almost immediately to begin laying the foundation for a full-scale adoption of a culture of experimentation and evaluation.

A useful first step would be to instill a culture of experimentation at OIRA itself. OIRA's guidance regarding the use of cost-benefit analysis in the construction and evaluation of regulation is encapsulated in its Circular A-4. Although this document emphasizes the importance of cost-benefit analysis, it provides little guidance on how to determine whether evidence is credible. It would be straightforward for OIRA to release a supplement to Circular A-4 detailing the virtues of experimental and quasi-experiment evaluations and setting out guidelines for the implementation of such evaluations.

Such a supplement could part ways from current guidance in a few respects. First, it could make clear that cost-benefit evaluations (especially prospective ones) are not enough to guarantee approval of a regulation. Rather, there must be a credible analysis following a trial period of small-scale implementation, or the promise of a credible future analysis, for approval to be granted. Second, the supplement could require that regulations be evaluated retrospectively, as well as prospectively. Third, it could encourage regulatory agencies to structure new regulations to allow for experimental or quasi-experimental evaluations.

VI. Will Experimentation and Evaluation Solve All Regulatory Problems?

Of course, the answer to this question is no. My proposal is best suited to addressing environmental, health, labor market, and safety regulations. However, the approach I have described is applicable in other areas as well. For example, Greenstone, Oyer, and Vissing-Jorgensen (2006) assess the benefits of mandatory disclosure regulations in financial markets. Similarly, Doidge, Karolyi, and Stulz (2008) provide evidence on the effects of the Sarbanes-Oxley Act, which regulates firms selling shares in the United States.

This proposal does not directly tackle issues of regulatory omission. However, it may have an indirect effect in this area. A system of regulatory experimentation and evaluation should provide lawmakers with enough confidence to try a wider range of potential regulations. With the assurance that ineffective regulations will be repealed, rather than lingering on the books for decades, lawmakers should feel more confident about experimenting.

Further, an occasional complaint about cost-benefit analysis is that the methodology is flawed. In particular, some critics argue that analysts have too much discretion in the calculations. I agree that the current approach offers too many opportunities for abuse. Experimentation will go a long way toward addressing this problem. With credible evaluations, it would be much more difficult to adjust cost-benefit analyses to fit ideological parameters.

VII. Conclusions

The current system of evaluating regulations prospectively means that we evaluate them when we know the least about their effectiveness. Real reform of regulation means introducing a culture of regulatory experimentation and evaluation. This essay has outlined a method to reform our system of regulation. It involves the four following simple steps.

1. **Experiment, Experiment, Experiment!** The key to a system of regulatory experimentation and evaluation is a process that accumulates credible evidence on regulations' costs and benefits. Such a system demands that regulations be structured at the outset so that they can be evaluated and that evaluations be fully funded.

2. **Create a Regulatory Review Board.** The board's task would be to assess the effectiveness of regulations and to repeal the ineffective ones.

3. **Automatic Sunset and Expansion Provisions.** The purpose of these provisions is to ensure that ineffective regulations are removed and that society fully benefits from the effective ones.

4. **Develop and Apply a Code of Ethics.** It is crucial to develop a code of ethics for regulatory experiments involving humans that ensures the subject's safety. Further, the federal government should create a board to ensure that all regulatory experiments are conducted ethically.

These four reforms have the potential to fundamentally alter the operation of our regulatory system. Just as we rely on the FDA to ensure that our foods and drugs pose no dangers, we should implement a regulatory system that yields safe and effective regulations.

We are entering a period where many of government's functions are being reconsidered. Such opportunities have appeared infrequently in American history. We must seize this opportunity to reform our regulatory system. In the process, we can improve our lives, our children's lives, and those of our children's children.

Notes

1 I thank James Block, Severin Borenstein, Jonathan Cedarbaum, John Cisternino, Ted Gayer, Sendhil Mullainathan, David Moss, Katherine Ozment, Mitchell Weiss, and the other authors of this volume for a series of insightful comments. Henry Swift provided outstanding research assistance.

2 There are several standard criticisms of cost-benefit analysis. They include the objections that it immorally commodifies objects (such as human life) that are beyond valuation, gives a false sense of scientific certainty, and unfairly benefits the rich. Several commentators, including Revesz and Livermore (2008) and Sunstein (2004), provide powerful responses to these criticisms. A rehashing of these arguments is beyond the scope of this paper, the primary argument of which is not that we should use cost-benefit analysis but that we should do it better and then follow its implications. For an excellent argument in favor of cost-benefit analysis, see Arrow *et al* (1996); this article includes eight principles on the appropriate use of benefit-cost analysis.

3 The term *de-identified data* refers to data from which all identifying information of subjects has been removed. It is crucial to protect the confidentiality of those who are selected to participate in any studies of regulatory effectiveness.

References

Arrow, Kenneth J., *et al.* "Is there a Role for Benefit-Cost Analysis in Environmental, Health, and Safety Regulation?" Science 272 (1996): 221–22.

Ashenfelter, Orley. "Estimating the Effect of Training Programs on Earnings." *Review of Economics and Statistics* 60, no. 1 (1978): 47–57.

Ashenfelter, Orley and David Card. "Using the Longitudinal Structure of Earnings to Estimate the Effect of Training Programs." *Review of Economics and Statistics* 67, no. 4 (1985): 648–60.

Doidge, Craig, G. Andrew Karolyi, and Rene M. Stulz. "Why Do Foreign Firms Leave U.S. Equity Markets? An Analysis of Deregistration Under SEC Exchange Act Rule 12h-6." NBER Working Paper no. 14245, 2008.

Greenstone, Michael and Justin Gallagher. "Does Hazardous Waste Matter? Evidence from the Housing Market and the Superfund Program." *Quarterly Journal of Economics* 123, no. 3 (2008): 951–1003.

Greenstone, Michael, Paul Oyer, and Annette Vissing-Jorgensen. "Mandated Disclosure, Stock Returns, and the 1964 Securities Act." *Quarterly Journal of Economics*, 121, no. 2 (2006): 399–460.

McCarthy, Tom. *Auto Mania: Cars, Consumers, and the Environment*. New Haven, CT: Yale University Press, 2007.

Morrall III, John F. "Saving Lives: A Review of the Record." *Journal of Risk and Uncertainty* 27, no. 3 (2003): 221–37.

Revesz, Richard L., and Michael A. Livermore. *Retaking Rationality: How Cost-Benefit Analysis Can Better Protect the Environment and Our Health*. Oxford: Oxford University Press, 2008.

Sunstein, Cass. "Your Money or Your Life." *The New Republic*, March 15, 2004: 27–30.

CHAPTER 6

The Promise and Pitfalls of Co-Regulation: How Governments Can Draw on Private Governance for Public Purpose

Edward J. Balleisen and Marc Eisner

Our purpose in this chapter is to examine the potential role of nongovernmental actors, and especially those with close connections to the business community, in fostering positive regulatory outcomes. Such an effort might well strike some readers as quixotic, in light of several recent regulatory fiascos. Consider the following tales of crisis born of regulatory failure, one from the world of finance, the other from the domain of environmental protection. Both occurred in 2008. Each involves a regulatory program that almost all Americans, and indeed quite possibly most members of Congress, had never heard of, at least before these spectacular demonstrations of insufficient regulatory oversight. Each also powerfully underscores the potential dangers associated with placing primary responsibility for regulating business in the hands of the business community itself—a strategy long known as "self-regulation."

The financial story concerns the collapse of three of America's largest investment banks, developments that sent shockwaves through the global financial system. Bear Stearns and Merrill Lynch were acquired at fire-sale prices by J. P. Morgan Chase and Bank of America, respectively, while Lehman Brothers entered bankruptcy. The downfalls of these pillars of Wall Street had numerous causes, but a particularly important one was their remarkable reliance on leverage, which in each case came to exceed thirty dollars of financial obligations to one dollar of capital, far beyond the ratios that bankers and regulators would have deemed prudent thirty years ago. Bank executives, and regulators at the Securities and Exchange Commission, assumed that such heightened debt exposure would prove perfectly safe, partly because of a new initiative, the Consolidated Supervised Entities (CSE) Program. The CSE delegated regulatory risk assessment to the investment banks themselves. The banks' risk managers, using their own highly sophisticated internal computer models, would continuously assess the risk associated with the bank's overall investment portfolio and debt obligations, and then require adjustments in capital whenever the risk assessment warranted. In late September of this year, after an intensive SEC autopsy of what had gone wrong at Bear Stearns, the chairman of the SEC, Christopher Cox, proclaimed that the CSE was "fundamentally flawed," and ordered its termination. Bear Stearns, it turns out, did regular risk assessments, but somehow never assessed the biggest risk faced by the firm—the impact that a sharp downturn in housing prices could have on its massive investments in mortgage-backed securities.[1]

The environmental story comes from eastern Tennessee. On December 22, after a series of heavy storms, an earthen dam gave way outside the small city of Kingston, releasing more than a billion gallons of toxic coal ash with dangerous concentrations of heavy metals. The Tennessee Valley Authority's nearby coal-fired power plant had sequestered the ash in the lagoon behind the dam. After the dam's collapse, a toxic stew containing 5.4 million cubic yards of coal ash inundated a portion of Roane County and contaminated a river coursing through a far larger region of Appalachia. Roughly eight years previously, the Environmental Protection Agency had been on the verge of issuing tough new rules about the handling and disposal of coal ash, because of growing scientific evidence that it poses serious threats to the quality of surrounding groundwater, and thus to human health. But confronted with intense opposition from electricity producers, including both privately owned utilities and publicly owned ones such as the TVA, the EPA backed off from adopting regulations that would have required much more costly measures to keep coal ash from leeching or cascading into the wider environment. During the Bush Administration, the EPA even shied away from issuing recommendations for state regulation of coal ash. Instead, it deferred to an "Action Plan" devised by the Utilities Solid Wastes Activity Group (USWAG), an organization of utilities that produce electricity from coal, and so must confront the vexing question of what to do with coal ash. The USWAG plan, which utilities could adopt voluntarily, called for a restricted set of standards for groundwater safety, occasional testing, and not much else. It completely skirted more expensive precautions such as linings for storage basins and reinforced dams. In early 2008, USWAG's executive director assured critics that "the utility companies want to do the right thing. They want to manage their ash so it won't have an adverse affect on human health and the environment." Such guarantees likely ring hollow to east Tennesseans whose houses now lie submerged under coal ash, or whose watersheds now have concentrations of arsenic that have increased more than a hundredfold.[2]

What lessons should legislators and regulators draw from such events? One of the authors of an essay in this volume, the economist Joseph Stiglitz, has not minced words in rendering his verdict on the CSE. "Self-regulation," he insists in a January 2009 reflection on the causes of the financial crisis, "is preposterous."[3] If we equate "self-regulation" with the sort of vaguely defined, poorly designed, feebly monitored, largely sanctionless, and voluntary institutions represented by the CSE program and the USWAG Action Plan, Stiglitz's judgment is surely correct.

But there are circumstances in which the state has delegated regulatory responsibilities to corporations, or to organizations affiliated with trade associations, with beneficial results. The problem often is not self-regulation *per se*, but the failure to integrate structures of private governance effectively within a larger institutional setting—to embed those structures within a broader framework of public oversight. In this chapter, we self-consciously use the term "co-regulation" to speak to the importance of integration and institutional design.

Governments across the globe have relied on private mechanisms of regulatory governance for decades, in a wide array of regulatory contexts. Such reliance almost always occurs at least partly as a means of reducing the public costs of regulation, and sometimes reflects rigid antagonism to the use of state power. But it can also emerge as a result of genuine concern for effective regulatory governance, and in some contexts, has actually furthered the common good. A burgeoning social-science literature has identified the key prerequisites for businesses and business-linked organizations to play constructive regulatory roles.[4] Private regulatory actors must possess genuine commitment to regulatory purposes, have a sufficient degree of institutional autonomy, and receive adequate resources to do their jobs properly. Equally important, they must be directed and constrained by a larger framework of "co-regulation." The state must furnish regulators with clear missions, and then maintain a close watch over those quasi-public or private regulators. To make such oversight efficacious, public regulators must receive accurate information about the activities of their private counterparts, and have sufficient expertise and capacity to assess the performance of nongovernmental regulators; and those nongovernmental regulators must face a credible threat that their public overseers will assume regulatory jurisdiction if they do not meet their obligations. It also helps if there is considerable transparency about the actions of quasi-public or private regulators that third parties can assist in the evaluation of regulatory performance. The key, in short, is to make sure that the private regulatory tail does not wag the commonweal's dog.

After briefly laying our conceptual and definitional groundwork, we explicate the most important principles of effective nongovernmental regulation. Since

American environmental regulation has generated several instructive experiments with private regulatory governance over the last generation, we then explore that history in some detail. Finally, we offer some suggestions for how our principles might guide regulatory policy with regard to the environment and oversight of the financial system. We choose these two regulatory contexts because private regulatory governance has long been a key feature of public policy in these arenas, and because their complexities makes them prime candidates for some delegation of regulatory authority, albeit as part of a larger system of co-regulation.

The Guises of Nongovernmental Regulation

Since the rise of the modern bureaucratic state, two distinct forms of private regulatory governance have arisen as adjuncts to public regulatory regimes. The first type vests the power to make and/or enforce regulatory rules in a nonprofit organization, usually allied to an industry trade association. Policymakers and academics frequently refer to these entities as "self-regulatory organizations," or SROs. Prominent American examples include the Joint Committee on the Accreditation of Healthcare Organizations, which certifies that medical providers qualify for government reimbursement programs, the Financial Industry Regulatory Authority, which oversees securities exchanges and licenses stockbrokers, and the Institute of Nuclear Power Operators, which sets safety standards for nuclear power plants and plays a key role in their inspection.

The second type, which among social scientists often goes by the name of "management regulation," involves analogous regulatory action within large-scale corporations, usually through the creation of internal regulatory departments, which have the responsibility of setting regulatory goals and overseeing their implementation. Amid all of the deregulation in the last two generations, this regulatory strategy has been embraced by such varied regulatory agencies as the Food and Drug Administration, the California Occupational Safety and Health Administration, and the Environmental Protection Agency. Many global corporations taking this path have done so at least in part to gain certification from the International Standards Organization (ISO), such that, with regard to a given aspect of their business (environmental stewardship, worker and product safety), they follow an identifiable set of socially advantageous managerial practices.

Regardless of whether private regulation is carried out by an SRO or a unit within a business firm, it can involve a range of regulatory functions and reflect a spectrum of coercive authority. Some nongovernmental regulators merely set standards; others primarily monitor regulatory compliance; still others enforce compliance; and yet still others perform all of these roles. In many instances, private governance has a wholly voluntary character, with firms possessing the choice of whether or not to commit themselves to regulatory rules and oversight. In other contexts, the state has conferred quasi-public status on SROs, requiring business participation. SROs with statutorily mandated authority often have the capacity to fine violators of regulatory rules or bar them from further activity in the marketplace. By contrast, voluntary SROs have far weaker enforcement powers, since American antitrust law prohibits such vigorous enforcement actions by trade associations. They can only wield the power of publicity, "naming and shaming" the violators of voluntary standards, or expelling them from participation in the industry group.

The Principles of Effective Co-Regulation

From the earliest years of the modern regulatory state, the call for private regulation has frequently served as a crucial tactic in the politics of deflection. Whenever some corner of the business community faces a groundswell of popular support for regulations that will impinge on its commercial practices, the odds are good that its leaders will champion some form of industry-wide regulatory self-governance as a means to forestall more onerous rule making and enforcement by the state. As cases like the CSE Program and the USWAG Action Plan reveal, private regulation can reflect little more than such efforts to keep the state at bay, with highly regrettable consequences for the wider society. But sometimes, enduring fear of intrusive state action, especially when accompanied by substantive public oversight and an ongoing desire to improve a firm's or industry's public standing, has prompted considerably more substantive responses from business. The effectiveness of private regulation in a particular context—or, more precisely, the potential for credible co-regulation—depends on the following five factors: (1) the depth of concern for their reputation among regulated businesses; (2) the relevance of flexibility in regulatory detail; (3) the existence of sufficient bureaucratic capacity and autonomy on the part of nongovernmental regulators; (4) the degree of transparency in regulatory process; and (5) the seriousness of accountability. Before legislators or regulatory agencies choose to delegate regulatory authority to industry organizations or corporations, they should assess the regulatory lay of the land with respect to each of these issues.

Identifying the Depth of Reputational Concern

One crucial factor in effective co-regulation is how much business leaders actually care about achieving regulatory objectives. Corporate executives, of course, have a fiduciary responsibility to look out for the interests of their shareholders. That responsibility frequently requires negotiation of a highly complex environment occupied by regulators, economic stakeholders such as customers, suppliers, insurers, and financiers, and social interests such as environmental groups and community organizations.[5] On some occasions, the search for profitability actually encourages a corporate embrace of regulatory goals, such as the reduction of environmental degradation or the diminution of negative impacts on health and safety. Although many businesses seek such ends primarily as a means of preventing regulatory fines and liabilities, others do so in the hopes of enhancing their reputation among key stakeholders. As an analysis of the adoption of environmental management systems by S&P 500 firms concluded that "while the potentially high costs of compliance with existing and anticipated regulations, as well as the threat of liabilities, are inducing firms to be more proactive about managing their environmental impacts, the direct effects of these pressures are not as strong as those of nonregulatory pressures from consumers, investors and communities."[6] Given the infrequency of regulatory inspections and fines, the emphasis placed on the larger set of actors in a corporation's organizational environment should come as no surprise. Yet, we must recognize that there is a wide range of activities in which firms may engage as they try to manage their reputations. At one end of the continuum, they may simply invest in public-relations efforts to create the *appearance* of social responsibility. At the other end of the continuum, they may make significant investments in redesigning products and processes, or they may even introduce internal management systems subject to external auditing, thereby going beyond regulatory requirements. The efficacy of co-regulation will depend on the extent to which it induces firms to move toward the maximal end of this continuum.

In recent decades, several trade associations have developed standards or model management systems for members, often in response to crises that threatened their collective reputations and raised the specter of impending regulation. Such activities can serve important functions: they can reduce the costs incurred by firms, create a context for industry actors to share information, and contribute to the development of an "industrial morality."[7] Moreover, if government and associations cooperate in the design of these systems, they can be integrated with regulation so that associations can serve, in effect, as surrogate regulators. But the existence of association codes or programs says little about their efficacy. If association programs are weak—that is, if they do not establish stringent expectations, require external auditing and information disclosure, and expel firms for noncompliance—they may invite problems of adverse selection. Firms with weak records may gravitate toward undemanding programs to enhance their reputations without changing their practices. This may create a Gresham's Law of self-regulation: weak participants drive out firms seeking to make credible efforts. Thus, the chemical industry's Responsible Care Program, which failed to eject members for noncompliance, tended to attract firms with worse-than-average pollution records (although there is evidence of improvement as of late). In contrast, the American Forest and Paper Association's Sustainable Forestry Initiative, which mandated external auditing and expelled members for noncompliance, attracted firms with stronger performance records.[8]

Reputational concerns that result from a particular crisis, of course, may lessen as media attention fades. The manufacturing firm that responds to negative publicity about its environmental impact with a high-powered public relations initiative or contributions to the Nature Conservancy may well soon turn its focus to the next advertising campaign. By contrast, if firms make the investments to gain ISO certification for their environmental management systems, or to meet demanding requirements imposed by a trade association, regulatory practices may take on a greater permanence. The creation of highly trained staffs and complex information management systems can generate internal momentum for regulatory action, which can be magnified by the need of companies to demonstrate certified compliance with standards or association codes to gain access to the supply chains and bid-lists of other organizations. Optimally, reputational concern triggers far-reaching transformation of how corporations design their products, processes, and facilities, and in the commercial relationships that they forge with a broad array of public and private stakeholders.

Regulatory policymakers, then, should be more willing to delegate regulatory authority to the business community when they see deep-seated concern about corporate standing with the public, manifested by the willingness to make considerable investments in internal regulatory capacity. And they should pay close attention to whether structures of countervailing economic power stand ready to help police regulatory behavior.

Ascertaining the Importance of Flexibility

Public regulators frequently confront daunting problems of information scarcity and complexity, even as they must cope with serious resource constraints. Ponder for a moment the dilemmas of the environmental or the safety regulator. If all regulated entities employed the same technologies, production processes, and inputs, environmental and safety agencies would have little difficulty in designing effective technology-based regulations. If this homogeneity is absent—as it commonly is—regulators might be able to employ performance-based regulations, assuming that they possessed the capacity to assess outputs. But sometimes low levels of homogeneity accompany a limited capacity to assess outcomes. In such instances, there is a strong case for management-based regulation, "which requires firms to engage in their own planning and internal rulemaking efforts that are supposed to aim toward the achievement of specific public goals."[9] By delegating authority to firms, the administrative state vests responsibility in the actors who possess the best information, thereby reducing the analytical and resource demands placed on regulators. In order to work, such approaches require that firms possess considerable flexibility, so that they can tailor internal regulatory systems to reflect the specific features of their firms and production processes. If successful, delegation can allow firms to go beyond what would be possible under traditional forms of regulation.

The delegation that is intrinsic to co-regulation creates a pair of related challenges for policymakers. First, as Cary Coglianese and David Lazer note, "the challenge for the regulator is . . . to find an optimal level of specificity that points firms in the right direction and enables inspectors to assess whether a firm has a good management system in place, but that also is not [so] specific that private managers no longer have the flexibility to adapt their practices to the individual conditions of their organizations."[10] Second, the architects of regulatory institutions must build in sufficient structures of accountability without simultaneously eliminating the incentives for participation. Delegation creates openings for miscommunication, shirking, and opportunistic behavior, vulnerabilities that grow under conditions of information scarcity and complexity. Regulatory design can limit such weaknesses by fostering increased transparency and accountability (this point will be developed in greater detail below). But regulatory policymakers should remain mindful of an unavoidable trade-off here. If these efforts dramatically increase regulatory transaction costs, they may create disincentives for potential participants.

Assessing the Prospects for Bureaucratic Capacity and Autonomy

In public policy, street-level bureaucrats are vitally important. To the extent that they fail to exercise their discretionary authority in a manner that reinforces the larger goals of policy, policy invariably fails. This observation holds as well for the private or quasi-public bureaucrats charged with critical responsibilities under strategies of co-regulation. A key question is whether corporations have the bureaucratic capacity, resources, and ethos necessary to implement regulatory schemes. Although large firms typically can call on sufficient administrative resources, the same cannot necessarily be said of small and medium-size enterprises (SMEs). To be effective participants in a system of co-regulation, corporations must be able to draw on personnel who grasp regulatory goals and who understand how their companies can achieve them. Business enterprises must have the flexibility to redesign products and processes, as well as the resources to implement the changes. They must have management systems in place to monitor performance, identify failures, and make necessary reforms. All of this can be difficult or impossible for SMEs. One study of enforced self-regulation of food safety, for example, concluded that SMEs routinely failed to develop dynamic management systems, were incapable of assessing their own compliance, and lacked knowledge of legal requirements. "Organizationally incompetent," these small-scale players in the food industry proved incapable of meeting their obligations.[11]

The difficulties noted above may not be simply a consequence of scale. Social scientists interested in corporate social responsibility have now demonstrated that firms engaging in socially responsible production are more profitable than firms that do not, but there is considerable uncertainty regarding the causes of this phenomenon.[12] In many instances, profitable firms may simply be the ones with sufficient resources to develop the kinds of management systems and routines that allow them to go beyond regulatory requirements in managing their environmental, safety, and health impacts. Thus the capacity for participation in co-regulation may often be contingent on corporate profitability and therefore vulnerable to the larger business cycle. Large firms operating on narrow profit margins may not be willing or able to make the investments that are essential for effective co-regulation.

The implications for policymakers are twofold. First, rather than viewing co-regulation as a universal solution, legislators and administrative officials must design processes and institutions that can differentiate among firms and industry associations, based on their organizational capacities and exhibited records of regulatory compliance. Policymakers must accordingly retain more traditional forms of regulation for firms or economic sectors that do not measure up to the prerequisites of self-governance. Secondly, if the ultimate goal is to extend some form of co-regulation to a broader subset of firms, it may be necessary to promote organizational change to create both the capacity for private governance and enduring commitment to regulatory aspirations.[13] The EPA has used various forms of outreach to educate corporate managers about how corporations have used environment management systems, design for environment, and green accounting to promote higher levels of environmental stewardship. Various trade associations have similarly employed peer auditing teams to convey effective strategies to association members seeking to build a capacity for internal regulatory governance. Such forms of support could prove critical to SMEs that lack the financial and analytical resources to achieve higher levels of regulatory compliance.

Ensuring Genuine Transparency

Like regulation carried out solely by governmental agencies, regulatory policy conceived and implemented by business organizations has to be visible to be effective. This principle has several dimensions. If regulatory goals are not defined with sufficient precision, we can hardly expect any regulatory agent, whether public or private, to attain them. The same point holds for regulatory objectives that lack at least roughly measurable benchmarks. Even with plainly articulated aims and consistently defined metrics, though, private regulatory efforts will likely devolve into public-relations exercises unless their outcomes consistently reach the light of day. At a minimum, the results of inspections and other forms of monitoring must flow up the regulatory chain, from inspectors to corporate compliance officers and/or the heads of enforcement at SROs, and from those self-regulatory institutions to public oversight bodies. And the resulting reports must come in a sufficiently standardized form, and reach sufficiently well-trained and well-resourced oversight personnel, that industry regulators and the government can actually assess regulatory consequences. Additionally, this information should be available to commercial counterparties like banks and insurance companies, and all interested nongovernmental organizations, in order to magnify the reputational and economic ramifications of poor performance.

Poor reporting standards and practices invariably translate into shoddy regulation—an unsurprising pattern exemplified by the implementation of the CSE program for investment banks. According the SEC's Inspector General's September 2008 report on the collapse at Bear Stearns, the firm's risk management team ignored numerous reporting requirements, but avoided even the most minor slap on the wrist for these transgressions.[14] Self-regulation, however, does not necessarily involve such regulatory malfeasance. In the wake of the near meltdown at Three Mile Island, for example, the Institute of Nuclear Power Operators (INPO) quickly developed a culture of information sharing, from individual plants to INPO, from INPO to the Nuclear Regulatory Commission, and from INPO back to individual plants. INPO's efforts included not only intensive dissemination of information about safety strategies that worked well, but also an annual meeting of plant executives in which the organization disclosed annual safety rankings for nuclear facilities, from top to bottom. This ritual at once reinforced industry-wide social norms about the centrality of safety and galvanized managers' competitive drive, alongside their perhaps even stronger desire to avoid losing face among their peers.[15]

Independent auditing of self-regulatory activities by third parties offers a further means of ensuring the trustworthiness and accuracy of data about regulatory outcomes. This strategy has proved especially valuable when the regulated entities are multinational corporations whose business endeavors (logging in rain forests, reliance on global supply chains) span a multitude of jurisdictional boundaries. Regardless of the geographic reach of an industry's businesses, transparent monitoring is an essential element of any strategy to create institutions of private governance that can actually attain society's regulatory objectives. Such monitoring, though, matters most when coupled with genuine oversight and enforcement.

Furnishing Mechanisms of Accountability

If SROs or schemes of management regulation are going to have more impact than simply forestalling more substantial action by the state, they must hold the economic actors in their jurisdiction to account, and simultaneously answer to governmental watchdogs that actually pay attention, and punish poor performance. SROs with statutory authority, such as the Financial Industry Regulatory Authority (formally the National Association of Securities Dealers), must have not just the power to levy fines or to take away the licenses of regulated firms that violate the rules, but also vigorous enforcement programs. Internal corporate regulators must possess authority that other departments within the enterprise are actually bound to respect.

It is at least equally important that public regulators keep a close eye on those charged with the responsibilities associated with regulatory self-governance, lest delegation degenerate into abdication. Governmental officials must regularly monitor self-regulatory activities, assess their performance, and, where appropriate, step in with more intrusive regulatory regimes, with their own rules and penalties. In some contexts, regulatory agencies might consider the creation of dual-track regulatory frameworks. Such two-tiered regulatory initiatives set performance floors, and then offer exemption from traditional regulatory inspections and enforcement regimes for firms that demonstrate the capacity to meet substantially higher standards through their own governance structures. Under such conditions, provisions for co-regulation are integrated into the regulatory structure and parties in the top tier have a clear sense that regulatory officials of the state stand ready, willing, and able to impose a traditional regulatory regime, if self-regulation fails to achieve public purposes.

Both the CSE Program and the USWAG initiative on the disposal of coal ash fell far short of these essential requirements. At Bear Stearns, for example, the risk management team was woefully understaffed, and lacked the authority to shape the day-to-day strategies of the traders with whom they worked side by side. For the CSE Program as a whole, the Trading and Markets Division had a mere seven inspectors to oversee the activities of investment banks that collectively controlled more than $4 trillion in assets. Despite these limitations, and the spotty record of reporting by the investment banks, the SEC's Division of Trading and Markets nonetheless had inklings of significant problems with internal regulatory structures at the investment banks. Yet instead of viewing themselves as obliged to step in to safeguard the public's interest, SEC officials consistently shied away from pressing the firm's executives or its risk managers to respond to these problems.[16] If anything, the USWAG approach to coal ash impoundment leaves even more to be desired. Industry's preferences here involve remarkably tepid standards, minimal private monitoring, a complete lack of tangible sanctions for utilities that do not live up to their professed responsibilities, and essentially no oversight role for the EPA or state environmental agencies.[17] Such forms of unmonitored or barely overseen self-regulation can only end in failure; regulatory policymakers should accordingly shun them.

Co-Regulation in Action: Environmental Policy Under Clinton and Bush

Environmental protection has proven to be an area ripe for co-regulation over the past generation, largely because of some significant limitations on key regulatory agencies. First, environmental statutes tend to be highly detailed, delegating minimal discretionary authority to the EPA. Given the sharp partisan conflicts of recent decades, there has been no substantial new environmental legislation since the Clean Air Act Amendments of 1990. Second, the EPA has functioned under extraordinary resource constraints. Its budget, adjusted for inflation, has not grown in the past three decades despite a more than doubling of the size of the U.S. economy. Third, from high-production-volume chemicals to emerging issues such as nanotechnology, the EPA is forced to manage levels of scientific complexity and uncertainty that are literally unparalleled in other regulatory arenas. Lacking the bureaucratic capacity and resources to develop the scientific and analytical foundations for new policy, the EPA frequently occupies an unenviable position. All of these constraints encouraged the delegation of considerable regulatory authority to private companies. The results reinforce key dimensions of our analysis.

In the 1990s, the Clinton administration responded to the constraints on environmental regulators by trying to "reinvent regulation," with the hope of promoting collaboration and fostering reliance on private-sector resources. Partners for the Environment, a collection of reinvention projects and partnerships, involved collaboration between the EPA and some eleven thousand organizations, including state and local regulators, corporations, trade and professional associations, and research institutions. Project XL (for "eXcellence and Leadership") emerged as the most important of the reinvention initiatives and made important steps toward meaningful co-regulation. Under Project XL, regulated entities were invited to submit proposals for innovative performance-based management systems. According to the EPA:

Participants are given the flexibility to develop common-sense, cost-effective strategies that will replace or modify specific regulatory requirements, on the condition that they produce greater environmental benefits. Based on the premise that these participants know better than the federal government how to reduce their pollution, Project XL reduces the regulatory burdens and promotes economic growth while achieving better environmental and public health protection.[18]

The EPA solicited proposals in the hope of initiating fifty pilot programs that could yield results broadly applicable to other regulated entities. Its review process was rigorous. The agency only considered applicants if they had a clean record of regulatory compliance, a detailed presentation of how their proposals would generate the expected results, and some guarantee that the outcomes would be superior to what would have been available under standard regulation. Once chosen, participants were required to submit voluminous documentation and evaluations, all of which were disseminated via the Internet.

On the face of things, Project XL appeared to incorporate all the key features of effective co-regulation: it delegated authority to firms with sufficient capacity, provided flexibility, and maintained high levels of accountability and transparency. And the program generated some impressive results, as indicated by the experience of Intel. Under Project XL, Intel set emissions targets for its Maricopa County facility relative to baseline levels permissible under the Clean Air Act. In some cases, these targets were quite ambitious (for example, 80 percent of the baseline for volatile organic compounds, 45 percent of the baseline for carbon monoxide, 8 percent of the baseline for particulate matter, and 5 percent of the baseline for sulfur dioxide). The chip maker remained well below the nine emissions targets, each of which was well below what would be acceptable under existing laws. Several other participants, such as Merck Pharmaceuticals, demonstrated comparable improvements in environmental performance. A report on Project XL by the Organization for Economic Cooperation and Development concluded that "Intel Corporation and Merck Pharmaceuticals both have exceeded by wide margin their initial targets for air emissions set out in their Project XL agreements."[19] Unfortunately, the application process was bedeviled by lengthy delays and high regulatory-transaction costs. The negotiations involving Intel spanned seventeen months and cost the firm some $588,000. While some companies were willing to accept the costs and delays, others withdrew otherwise promising applications.[20] Moreover, many business leaders worried that Project XL did not provide sufficient latitude for innovation, even as many regulators found the program difficult to reconcile with the EPA's bureaucratic culture.[21]

The Bush administration retained numerous Clinton-era regulatory partnerships and created many new ones. In a few cases, these efforts have clearly borne fruit. For instance, the HPV (High Production Volume) Chemical Challenge Program enlisted corporations to collect toxicological data on chemicals, thereby supplementing the EPA's database without having to work through the cumbersome provisions of the Toxic Substances Control Act.[22] But in most of the Bush-era partnerships, members simply pledged that they would cooperate in the promotion of environmentally friendly practices. Some corporations went so far as to submit estimates of their accomplishments, but because these programs were not integrated into the regulatory structure and the results were unaudited, it is difficult to evaluate whether they in fact contributed to gains in environmental quality. These efforts certainly did not constitute examples of co-regulation.

In contrast to these partnerships, the National Environmental Performance Track (or NEPT) appears to hold greater promise. NEPT is an environmental green track, or alternative regulatory framework, based on the experiences gained from state-level green tracks and experiments in EPA Region 1 (New England). The EPA admits organizations to NEPT if they employ a high-quality environmental management system (EMS) assessed by third-party auditors using the EPA's assessment protocol, have a demonstrated commitment to continuous improvement, and have a strong record of compliance. The benefits of participation include: greater flexibility in compliance, streamlined permitting and reporting requirements, a lower inspection priority, and public recognition.[23] It is important to note that with NEPT, the EPA introduced co-regulation as a supplement to traditional forms of regulation that remained in place for firms not admitted to the green track. By the end of 2008, NEPT claimed 547 members, including such major corporations as 3M, Andersen Corporation, Bristol-Meyers Squibb, Coca-Cola, Hewlett-Packard, Intel, Johnson & Johnson, Monsanto, and Xerox, as well as large-scale public entities such as military bases. According to the EPA, NEPT members have reduced water use by 3.66 billion gallons, reduced greenhouse gas emissions by over 300,000 metric tons of carbon dioxide equivalents, reduced hazardous wastes by more than 52,000 tons, and realized impressive increase in the use of recycled materials.[24] The ultimate impact of NEPT, of course, might seem to be subject to significant constraints. It extends co-regulation to a relatively limited universe of organizations (both private and public sector) that have a demonstrated commitment to, and capacity for, genuine internal regulatory governance. But this is what we would expect: co-regulation is not a universal response to circumscribed regulatory capacity.

Future Directions for Policy—Co-Regulation and the Environment

The record of private regulatory initiatives in environmental policy suggests several potential avenues for the nation's regulatory agenda. Most obviously, we must recognize that the proliferation of partnerships at the EPA and the lack of institutional integration in the agency have been products, in part, of the difficulties of negotiating the cumbersome requirements of key statutes that simultaneously limit bureaucratic discretion and fail to provide regulators with the tools they need to execute their duties. Consider the Toxic Substances Control Act.[25] Under section 6 of TSCA, the EPA is authorized to regulate the manufacture, processing, distribution, use, or disposal of existing chemicals if it has determined that they pose an "unreasonable" risk to human health or the environment. It can also ban existing chemicals, but it bears the burden of proving that chemicals will present an unreasonable risk, that the agency has adopted the least burdensome regulatory response, and that the benefits of a ban outweigh the costs. Since the passage of this legislation in 1976, the EPA's regulatory efforts have been hamstrung by the failure of Congress to explicitly define what constitutes "unreasonable" risk. Moreover, the agency has encountered profound difficulties in accessing sufficient information to substantiate the determination of risk, the efficacy of substitutes, and the economic impacts of the regulatory response. Accordingly, it should come as no surprise that the majority of existing chemicals have not undergone basic toxicological testing.[26] TSCA section 4 authorizes the EPA to promulgate rules requiring testing for environmental and health effects for new and existing chemicals. Yet, in a regulatory catch-22, such rules must be justified with findings regarding production, exposure, and potentially unreasonable levels of risk that are difficult to substantiate without the very data that the rules would generate. Without the statutory authority to mandate information disclosure, the EPA has been forced to rely on partnerships and corporate voluntarism. Congress should accordingly revise TSCA and other key statutes to give the EPA the basic tools it needs to execute its regulatory duties.

The revision of key environmental statutes, of course, can be a difficult and time-consuming task. But there are less contentious reforms that could strengthen the incentives for sensible environmental co-regulation, such as participation in NEPT. First, and most importantly, new legislation should mandate the disclosure of audited environmental data for all firms, using standard metrics. At present, many firms have the leeway to gild their reputations for environmental stewardship through astute public relations because stakeholders rarely have access to high-quality information about environmental performance. In those instances in which corporations furnish data about that performance, they too often present it with a bewildering array of metrics and baselines that make meaningful comparisons difficult. Mandatory disclosure of standardized information about environmental impacts, akin to the publication of financial data that the Securities and Exchange Commission requires of public companies, would force a higher level of corporate accountability, particularly if combined with summary statistics for the top quartile of firms in a given industry. Such disclosure would create far stronger incentives for firms and trade associations to adopt credible management systems designed to reduce environmental impacts. The influence of the Toxic Release Inventory on corporate behavior provides clear evidence that what gets measured gets managed, so long as the public has ready access to the relevant data.[27]

Second, NEPT has proven itself to be an important innovation at EPA, justifying efforts to strengthen it and expand its reach. At present, NEPT requires that participants have a high-quality environmental management system (EMS), but the EPA has failed to require certification under ISO 14001—the global EMS standard—as a requirement for entry. This reticence is peculiar on several counts. EPA was intimately involved with the development of ISO 14001 (an EPA official co-chaired the Technical Committee responsible for developing this code). Moreover, ISO 14001 certification has become an increasingly important prerequisite for accessing global supply chains, and several studies have found that such certification correlates with the positive environmental performance. In the past decade, some trade associations have strengthened their own EMS codes to bring them into compliance with ISO 14001 (for example, the American Chemistry Council took this step in 2002, through changes in Responsible Care). Integrating ISO 14001 into NEPT would reinforce these trends, while reducing the regulatory transaction costs associated with entry, insofar as each EMS would not have to be examined *de novo*.

Third, and finally, the incentives for participation in NEPT and certification under ISO 14001 could be enhanced through government procurement practices. A series of executive orders beginning with EO 12873 (1993) and culminating in EO 13424 (2007) have promoted environmentally preferable purchasing. President Bush's EO 13424, for example, instructed the head of each agency to "require in agency acquisitions of goods and services (i) use of sustainable environmental practices, including acquisition of bio-based, environmentally preferable, energy-efficient, water-efficient, and recycled-content products, and (ii) use of paper of at least 30 percent post-consumer fiber content" (section 2). A new executive order could reinforce co-regulation by explicitly requiring that the government accord procurement preferences to businesses that participate in NEPT and/or are certified under ISO 14001. Since the United States government is the world's single largest consumer of goods and services, this simple change in procurement practices—if rigorously enforced—could have a transformative effect on association codes, corporate environmental management, and participation in the EPA's National Environmental Performance Track. It would likely also trigger similar shifts in procurement requirements by many states and municipalities.

Insofar as these changes create greater incentives for credible co-regulation, they will contribute to gains in environmental quality by engaging a broader field of forces, including markets, supply chains, and government procurement. By reducing the demands placed on regulators, such reforms can free up scarce resources that can be focused more effectively on helping firms build a capacity for internal regulatory governance, as well as identifying and sanctioning recalcitrant businesses that currently believe (and not without reason) that the low probability of inspection allows them to pollute with few consequences.

Future Directions for Policy—
Co-Regulation and the Financial System

Over the next few years, Congress and the regulatory agencies with authority over the financial sector are exceedingly likely to embark on far-reaching reforms. Prevailing proposals range from adoption of new substantive constraints on financial companies, such as tougher limits on leverage and firm size, tighter rules on executive compensation, and requirements that bond rating be insulated from conflicts of interest, to requirements that financial firms trade complex derivatives in standardized forms on public exchanges, much tighter enforcement of existing and new regulations through beefed-up budgets for administrative agencies, and fundamental structural reorganization of the regulatory agencies charged with ongoing rule-making and enforcement. Within this large and complex agenda for change, policymakers will have to come terms with the roles that industry self-policing will play in the new regulatory architecture.

In light of the profound failure of schemes such as the CSE program, there will be a strong temptation to look askance at any regulatory role for financial firms or nongovernmental organizations. But we would argue that the question ought not to be whether the American state should defer to self-regulation—that path leads at best to unmet public goals, and at worst to crisis and disaster. Rather, policymakers should ask whether they ought, in at least some areas, to strengthen institutions of co-regulation. Even with substantial increases in regulatory budgets, the American state is unlikely to fill every regulatory niche required by America's exceedingly complex financial system.

Three areas especially call out for attention here. One involves the parts of the securities markets where private governance already plays a central role— the stock and futures exchanges, FINRA's regulation of stockbrokerages, and the Financial Accounting Standards Board's formulation of guidance for corporate accounting. The SEC and Congressional oversight committees should undertake a fresh examination of FINRA's and FASB's regulatory performance, considering whether current arrangements sufficiently meet the requirements of meaningful co-regulation. The Bernard Madoff scandal certainly raises troubling questions about the degree to which FINRA, and before it NASD, was fulfilling its obligations to oversee the activities of broker-dealers during the past two decades. NASD officials inspected Madoff's firm periodically over that time frame, yet at no point uncovered the practices that eventually grew into a multibillion-dollar Ponzi scheme. The disastrous consequences resulting from such apparently kid-glove treatment of a prominent NASD leader suggests one obvious point of departure for reassessing the functioning of the financial sector's quasi-public and private regulators. Whether such reassessment comes from the SEC, or through the auspices of congressional hearings, investigators should surely ask whether these regulators continued to manifest a genuine concern for the financial markets' reputation for probity, a concern quite evident in the two generations following the Great Depression and the New Deal; whether they have been meeting the requirements of meaningful transparency; and to what extent their focus on accountability gave way before the rampant cronyism of the last decade.

A second area concerns some key financial intermediaries—mortgage brokers, investment advisers, and hedge funds—whose behavior contributed to the current financial crisis. Mortgage brokers directed hundreds of thousands of Americans into dangerous loans, often in order to maximize their own commissions; investment advisers steered tens of thousands of investors into risky securities like collateralized debt obligations (CDOs) without sufficient attention to the attendant risks; hedge funds plowed money into CDOs and other even more exotic financial instruments such as credit default swaps, oblivious to the implications for systemic financial stability. There is a growing consensus in favor of heightened federal regulation over all of these economic players. A strategy of co-regulation might especially make sense in the case of mortgage brokers and investment advisers, given the structural parallels between them and stockbrokerages. Dispersed throughout the entire country, and reflecting great diversity in scale and forms of business organization, these intermediaries might lend themselves to at least partial oversight by newly created SROs, in line with the advantages of regulatory flexibility. The alternative of traditional administrative regulation will surely confront daunting problems of monitoring and regulatory coverage.

Finally, policymakers might wish to think through the advantages and disadvantages of creating a quasi-public, nongovernmental institution to oversee the process of bond rating, which appears to have been thoroughly corrupted by conflicts of interest. The staffing and funding of such an institution would, no doubt, pose great challenges of regulatory design, as would the creation of opportunities for public input into setting standards and devising mechanisms of oversight by the relevant regulatory agencies. But this approach would seem to offer one way to avoid endemic conflicts of interest, while keeping the government out of the business of ranking the relative risk associated with various securities.

The financial scandals of the past several years, along with heightened public support for stricter regulation of the financial markets, improves the chances for crafting strategies of co-regulation that make a difference. The historical record, both within and outside the realm of finance, suggests that industries beset by crisis, especially crisis that has sullied their standing with the public, frequently prove more committed to building regulatory institutions that actually achieve their goals. That same record makes clear that to be effective, private regulatory governance must confront the scrutiny of an engaged and properly resourced regulatory state.[28] With attention to the right principles of design, targeted co-regulation might help American policymakers recreate the basic culture of trust so crucial to modern financial markets.

Co-Regulation As Policy Tool

We began this essay with two brief vignettes about regulatory failure. The victims of the credit crisis and the environmental disaster in eastern Tennessee now look to Washington policymakers for solutions. One could certainly forgive those policymakers for looking at a broken dam and a crippled financial system and concluding that self-regulation necessarily translates into no regulation at all. To be sure, proponents of private regulatory structures all too often design them in a haphazard and cavalier fashion, or embrace them as part of a larger political agenda that rejects a positive role for regulation. Corporations have a powerful incentive to maximize profits and, absent the constraints imposed by regulatory policy, many firms will, sooner or later, impose large and tragic costs on society. Given the stakes, reliance of any kind on private regulation might seem just too risky.

Yet there is powerful evidence that in the right circumstances, and with the right execution, strategies that incorporate private governance can extend the reach of regulation to areas that are simply beyond the analytical and budgetary capabilities of public regulators. Legislators and administrative agencies should view nongovernmental regulation as a policy instrument that can make sense in many, if by no means all, regulatory contexts. The key challenge is to design systems that provide the benefits of self-governance without sacrificing the high levels of accountability that one expects from public regulation.

We have argued that the substantial advantages of regulatory delegation, either to SROs or individual corporations, can result if and only if such delegation occurs within a larger system of co-regulation. The government must design regulatory institutions to ensure that the flexibility for internal regulation is extended only to organizations with the requisite capacity and expertise; it must simultaneously take great care to maximize transparency and accountability. If implemented with care, a regime of co-regulation can extend the capacity of public regulators to promote the public interest. It can harness reputational concerns, market and supply-chain forces, and the capabilities of trade and standards-setting organizations to achieve goals that are currently beyond the reach of public regulators. Co-regulation, if it represents ingenuity in policy design and dedication to sustained oversight, can mean smarter regulation, and better government.

Obviously, our conclusions give rise to many more specific questions, in each of the thematic areas that we have examined. How should we go about distinguishing genuine regulatory concern from a politically savvy charade? What degree of heterogeneity among regulated entities should trigger the search for regulatory delegation to nonstate actors? What kinds of management systems and corporate compliance departments are necessary to assure that an SRO or a corporation has the capacity, and the dedication, to participate in co-regulation? What quantity, and quality, of information disclosure will meet the demands of transparency? How should public regulators devise metrics or baselines for such corporate reporting, so as to ensure comparability of results? When, precisely, does monitoring and enforcement by private regulatory actors, or the oversight of those actors by public officials, attain a sufficient standard of accountability? The answers to these questions will inevitably vary across regulatory domains. Prerequisites for effective co-regulation in food safety, for example, will surely differ considerably from what is required in environmental management or finance. As such, they deserve careful consideration from scholars in every relevant social science discipline, as well as from the representatives of trade associations and public interest groups, and from analysts within regulatory agencies, the Office of Management and Budget, and congressional committees responsible for regulatory oversight.

What we propose here, then, is neither a blueprint nor a formula. Instead, we offer a analytical framework—some broad principles and key questions— that should help legislators and regulatory officials sensibly choose when to give representatives of business some measure of regulatory authority, and think more systematically about the need to integrate these efforts into a system of co-regulation. Policymakers must approach any potential reliance on nongovernmental regulatory structures with open eyes and an appreciation for the challenges of making them work. Legislators and bureaucrats cannot take corporate commitment to regulatory purposes for granted, even as they should not presume that any profession of such commitment is necessarily a mere smokescreen. They cannot approach co-regulation in the hope of discovering a cost-free solution—governments cannot create meaningful disclosure, much less meaningful accountability, without significant expenditure of resources. They further cannot assume that a given framework of co-regulation, once sensibly created, will achieve its goals without serious, consistent oversight. There is simply no regulatory free lunch.

Notes

1   "Chairman Cox Announces End of Consolidated Supervised Entities Program," Press Release, Securities and Exchange Commission, September 26, 2008, available at http://www.sec.gov/news/press/2008/2008-230.htm, accessed December 31, 2008; Office of Inspector General, U. S. Securities and Exchange Commission, *SEC's Oversight of Bear Stearns and Related Entities: The Consolidated Supervised Entity Program* (Washington, D. C., 2008); Stephen Labaton, "Agency's '04 Rule Let Banks Pile up New Debt," *The New York Times*, October 3, 2008: A1.

2   Earth Justice, "Comments on the Utility Solid Waste Activities Group's 'Utility Industry Action Plan for the Management of Coal Combustion Products,'" Pursuant to EPA Notice of Data Availability, August 29, 2007, Submitted January 28, 2008, available at http://www.earthjustice.org/library/references/noda_appendix_-d.pdf, accessed January 5, 2009; "Tennessee: Early Warnings on Ash Pond Leaks," *Chatanooga Times Free Press*, January 5, 2009, available at http://timesfreepress.com/news/2009/jan/05/tennessee-early-warnings-ash-pond-leaks/?local, accessed January 7, 2009; Shaila Dewan, "Hundreds of Coal Ash Dumps Lack Regulation," *The New York Times*, January 7, 2009: A1. Quote from Steve Mocarsky, "Health Risk from Fly Ash Dumping Debated: Environmentalist: Stricter Rules, Fed Oversight Needed. Utility Spokesman Disagrees," available at http://dev.centreforenergy.com/NewsMarkets/displayNewsArticle.asp?From=NewsSearch&Search=&NumberStoriesToDisplay=ALL&ResultCategoryType=2,3&NewsPageID=5&NewsID=9992359&template=2,3&currPage=13, accessed January 21, 2009.

3   Joseph Stiglitz, "Capitalist Fools," *Vanity Fair* (January 2009), available at http://www.vanityfair.com/magazine/2009/01/stiglitz200901, accessed January 9, 2009.

4   For especially useful overviews of this literature, *see* John Braithwaite, "Enforced Self-Regulation: A New Strategy for Corporate Crime Control," *Michigan Law Review* 80 (1982): 1466–1507; Neil Gunningham and Joseph Rees, "Industry Self-Regulation: An Institutional Perspective," *Law and Policy* 19 (1997): 363–414; Marc Eisner, "Corporate Environmentalism, Regulatory Reform, and Industry Self-Regulation: Toward Genuine Regulatory Reinvention in the United States," *Governance* 17 (2004): 146–67; and Edward J. Balleisen, "The Prospects for Effective 'Co-Regulation' in the United States: A Historian's View from the Early Twenty-

First Century," in *Government and Markets: Toward a New Theory of Economic Regulation*, edited with David Moss (Cambridge: Cambridge University Press, forthcoming 2009).

5   *See* Amy J. Hillman and Gerald D. Keim, "Shareholder Value, Stakeholder Management, and Social Issues: What's the Bottom Line? *Strategic Management Journal* 22, no. 2 (2001): 125–39; and Benjamin Cashore and Ilan Vertinsky, "Policy Networks and Firm Behaviours: Governance Systems and Firm Responses to External Demands for Sustainable Forest Management," *Policy Sciences* 33 (2000): 1–30.

6   Madhu Khanna and William Rose Q. Anton, "Corporate Environmental Management: Regulatory and Market-Based Incentives," *Land Economics* 78, no. 4 (November 2002): 555.

7   Neil Gunningham and Joseph Rees, "Industry Self-Regulation" (*see* note 4 above).

8   Michael J. Lennox and Jennifer Nash, "Industry Self-Regulation and Adverse Selection: A Comparison Across Four Trade Association Programs," *Business Strategy and the Environment*, 12 (2003): 343–56. *See also* Andrew A. King and Michael J. Lenox, "Industry Self-Regulation Without Sanctions: The Chemical Industry's Responsible Care Program," *Academy of Management Journal*, 43, no. 4 (2000): 698–716.

9   Cary Coglianese and David Lazer, "Management-Based Regulation: Prescribing Private Management to Achieve Public Goals," *Law & Society Review* 37, no. 4 (December 2003): 692. This discussion follows the argument presented by Coglianese and Lazer.

10 Ibid., 715.

11 Robyn Fairman and Charlotte Yapp, "Enforced Self-Regulation, Prescription, and Conceptions of Compliance within Small Businesses: The Impact of Enforcement," *Law and Policy* 27, no. 4 (October 2005): 504, 516. *See also* John Braithwaite, "Enforced Self-Regulation" (*see* note 4 above). He argues: "For businesses below a certain size, a viable and independent compliance unit is impossible. Direct government inspections must be retained for small businesses. In particular, government inspectors would continue to have a vital role in catching fly-by-night operators who calculatedly operate on the fringe of the law" (1501).

12 *See* Jean B. McGiorie, Alison Sundgren, and Thomas Schneeweis, "Corporate Social Responsibility and Firm Financial Performance," *Academy of Management Journal* 31, no. 4 (1988): 854–52; and Ronald M. Roman, Sefa Hayibor, and Bradley R. Agle, "The Relationship Between Social and Financial Performance: Repainting a Portrait," *Business & Society* 38, no. 1 (1999): 109–25.

13 *See* Andrew Hopkins, "Beyond Compliance Monitoring: New Strategies for Safety Regulators," *Law & Policy* 29, no. 2 (April 2007): 210–27.

14 *SEC's Oversight of Bear Stearns and Related Entities* (*see* note 1 above).

15 Joseph Rees, *Hostages of Each Other: The Transformation of Nuclear Safety since Three Mile Island* (Chicago: University of Chicago Press, 1994).

16 *SEC's Oversight of Bear Stearns and Related Entities* (*see* note 1 above).

17 In twenty-three states that prohibit state environmental agencies from adopting standards that are tougher than those required by the federal EPA, state regulation of fly ash lagoons is particularly limited. *See* Earth Justice, "Comments on the Utility Solid Waste Activities Group's 'Utility Industry Action Plan'" (*see* note 2 above); The Utility Solid Waste Activities Group, *et al*, "Comments on Notice of Data Availability on the Disposal of Coal Combustion Wastes in Landfills and Surface Impoundments, Pursuant to EPA Notice of Data Availability," August 29, 2007, submitted February 11, 2008, available at http://www.uswag.org/pdf/2008/NODAComments.pdf, accessed January 5, 2009.

18 U.S. Environmental Protection Agency, *Partners for the Environment: A Catalogue of the Agency's Partnership Programs* (Washington, DC: Environmental Protection Agency): 41.

19 OECD Working Party on National Environmental Policy, "Voluntary Approaches: Two United States Cases—The Experience of Intel Corporation and Merck Pharmaceuticals in Project XL." ENV/EPOC/WPNEP(2002)11/FINAL, January 8, 2003: 9.

20 Ibid., 22.

21 *See* Allen Blackman, James Boyd, Alan Krupnick, and Janice Mazurek, "The Economics of Tailored Regulation and the Implications for Project XL" (Washington, DC: Resources for the Future, 2001); and Alfred A. Marcus, Donald A. Geffen, and Ken Sexton, *Reinventing Environmental Regulation: Lessons from Project XL* (Washington, DC: Resources for the Future, 2002).

22 *See* Marc Allen Eisner, *Governing the Environment: The Transformation of Environmental Regulation* (Boulder, CO: Lynne Rienner, 2007): 185–88, 193–95.

23 *See* U.S. Environmental Protection Agency, *National Environmental Performance Track: Program Guide* (Washington, DC: Environmental Protection Agency, 2001). *See also* Eisner, *Governing the Environment*, 188–93 (*see* note 22 above).

24 This data is taken from http://www.epa.gov/performancetrack/index.htm (accessed December 29, 2008).

25 Lynn L. Bergeson, Lisa M. Campbell, and Lisa Rothenberg, "TSCA and the Future of Chemical Regulation," *EPA Administrative Law Reporter* 15, no. 4 (2000): 1–23.

26 Environmental Protection Agency, *Chemical Hazard Data Availability Study: What Do We Really Know About the Safety of High Production Volume Chemicals?* (Washington, DC: Environmental Protection Agency, 1998).

27 *See* Archon Fung and Dara O'Rourke, "Reinventing Environmental Regulation from the Grassroots Up: Explaining and Expanding on the Success of the Toxic Release Inventory," *Environmental Management* 25, no. 2 (2000): 115–27; and Mary Graham and Catherine Miller, "Disclosure of Toxic Releases in the United States," *Environment* 43, no. 8 (2001): 8–20.

28 For more extended discussion of these historical patterns, *see* Balleisen, "Prospects for Effective 'Co-Regulation'" (*see* note 4 above).

CHAPTER 7

The Principles of Embedded Liberalism: Social Legitimacy and Global Capitalism

Rawi Abdelal and John G. Ruggie

In this essay we revisit the principles of "embedded liberalism" and argue for their relevance to the contemporary global economy. The most essential principle is the need for markets to enjoy social legitimacy, because their political sustainability ultimately depends on it. From this principle we analyze three current sets of practices and institutions in which ongoing crises of legitimacy demonstrate the need for a renewal of embedded liberalism and a revitalization of global governance. They are: the activities of transnational corporations, particularly with regard to core standards in labor and human rights; the organization of the international financial architecture; and the formal rules and informal norms of international organizations.

Learning the Lessons of Embedded Liberalism

The post-1945 world economy embodied a social bargain. In the aftermath of the political and economic chaos of 1920s, the Great Depression of the 1930s, and the Second World War—all of which together shattered the world order within the span of a single generation—policymakers sought to reorganize and rebuild the world economy by restoring open markets, promising to mitigate their adverse social consequences and thereby preempting societal demands, from both left and right, to replace markets altogether. The failure to strike such a compromise earlier had undermined international cooperation in trade and macroeconomic policy during the 1920s and 1930s, just as it had caused the collapse of the first era of globalization, circa 1870 to 1914.

Influential scholars and policymakers began to make sense of how that first era of globalization had lost its way. In his 1944 book, *The Great Transformation*, Karl Polanyi distinguished "embedded" from "disembedded" economic orders. On Polanyi's reading of history, economic orders had always reflected the principles and values of the societies in which they were situated. Only in the middle of the nineteenth century was the idea of an economy that was somehow separate from society, a collection of markets with its own inexorable principles and logic, invented and then cultivated. This idea, which informed classical liberalism, was not only new but revolutionary. Whereas previous economic orders had always been "embedded" in social and political relations, this new liberalism succeeded in "disembedding" first national markets and, soon thereafter, cross-border markets, and ultimately global markets as well. Several policy practices were essential to this process of disembedding markets, above all the free movement of goods, services, and capital among nations.

The outbreak of war in 1914 led the combatant governments to suspend the convertibility of their currencies into gold and, often, into other currencies also. Fixed exchange rates, international commerce, and cross-border investment collapsed. In the early 1920s, European governments sought in vain to reestablish on the old principles of classical liberalism the prewar system in political circumstances that were much changed. Europe's continental empires had disintegrated into successor states whose governments often carefully guarded their economic autonomy. The working classes, long disenfranchised, empowered the left and politicized macroeconomic policymaking for the first time. Factories had been destroyed, public finances ruined, and currencies debauched throughout the continent. Germany struggled to make a success of the Weimar Republic's fragile democracy, but soon veered to the far right. The United States declined the opportunity of world leadership and withdrew instead into isolation. Russia was preoccupied by its Bolshevik Revolution, and Japan soon turned to militarism.

When U.S. and European policymakers, among them the great British economist John Maynard Keynes, began to debate the rules by which the international economy ought to be reconstructed, they agreed with the basic insight articulated by Polanyi: the disembedding of markets had been politically unsustainable. Simply put, national societies rejected laissez-faire; across widely varying political spectra, the first era of globalization had come to be seen as illegitimate by all segments of society, save possibly the bankers. Thus this most important lesson was drawn: markets that societies do not recognize as legitimate cannot last. So, policymakers set out to make sure that, this time around, cross-border markets would be more acceptable to the people who worked (and lived) within them and voted for the politicians who would regulate them. Markets would be reconciled with the values of social community and domestic welfare.

The formulation in a 1982 article by one of the authors of the present essay, John G. Ruggie, has become the dominant interpretation of the postwar international economy: a reconciliation of market and society termed *the compromise of embedded liberalism.* "Unlike the economic nationalism of the thirties, it would be multilateral in character; unlike the liberalism of the gold standard and free trade, its multilateralism would be predicated upon domestic interventionism." The practices of domestic interventionism would tame the socially disruptive effects of markets without, however, eliminating the welfare and efficiency gains derived from cross-country trade. National societies shared the risks through varieties of safeguards and insurance schemes that composed, in part, the European welfare states or, in the ever-exceptional United States, the New Deal state. Sophisticated modeling has demonstrated that embedded liberalism generated both better long-term economic performance and social protection than its laissez-faire predecessor.

In that same article, Ruggie conjectures that "the resurgent ethos of liberal capitalism"—what later became known as neoliberalism—threatened to undo the compromise of embedded liberalism as the world had known it. In the event, it wasn't merely embedded liberalism's specific policy tools that became discredited; its paradigm of political economy was itself attacked and undermined. An analysis of the specifics of this shift in thought is not essential to our learning the lessons of the era of embedded liberalism, circa 1945 to 1985. What is important is recognizing that our current era of globalization and its neoliberal paradigm have reached the point themselves of suffering from a profound crisis of legitimacy. If that crisis is not resolved by deft policymaking in the United States and around the world, globalization is likely to be undone by national policy reactions driven by societies that have grown increasingly skeptical of newly disembedded global markets. Policymakers must recognize, moreover, that this crisis of legitimacy for globalization has been unfolding since the end of the 1990s. The crash of 2008 did not cause this crisis, but has surely made it worse.

We therefore propose that policymakers revisit the principles of embedded liberalism in the hopes of embedding, and thereby legitimating, the practices of transnational corporations, the governance of financial markets, and the rules of international organizations. The core principle of embedded liberalism is the need to legitimize international markets by reconciling them to social values and shared institutional practices. This principle implies the need to bridge gaps in the governance of firms that produce, buy, and sell around the world, firms whose rights have in effect in the recent era of globalization outstripped the global frameworks that should regulate them. This principle further implies the need to balance, both domestically and internationally, the benefits of internationalized financial markets with their substantial risks; to share the rewards and costs of the disruptions created by internationalized markets across national

societies; and to ensure that global governance is based on multilateral delibera-
tion among countries whose leaders believe that the influence of their voices
reflects their place in a multipolar—or at least "nonpolar"—world.

Embedding the Activities of Transnational Corporations

The most visible institutional expression of globalization today is the transnational corporation (TNC). TNCs number approximately 77,000, with 800,000
subsidiaries and millions of suppliers. Critics in the industrialized countries
blame TNCs for exporting jobs to poorer countries with lower labor costs and
weaker protective regimes for labor, and for driving down the wages of workers
whose jobs are not exported. In the developing world, TNCs are frequently
seen as engaging in social and environmental practices they could never get away
with back home, because they are too powerful for capital-poor governments to
challenge. While containing elements of truth, both views are stereotypes. Of
course, even flawed perceptions can drive policy—in the case of TNCs typically
in a populist/economic nationalist direction.

Yet the fundamental challenge for the social legitimacy of TNCs is rooted
not in these shifting perceptions, but in an underlying institutional reality.
While the legal rights enabling TNCs to operate globally have expanded
significantly over the past generation, their activities are not adequately encompassed by global regulatory frameworks. This results in growing governance
gaps—between the scope and impact of their activities, and the capacity of
societies to manage their adverse consequences.

The more than 2,500 bilateral investment treaties currently in effect are a
case in point, the vast majority of which were adopted in the 1990s. While providing legitimate protection to foreign investors, these treaties also permit those
investors to take host states to binding international arbitration, not only for
expropriation but also for a variety of alleged damages resulting from the
implementation of legislation to improve domestic social and environmental
standards—even when the legislation applies uniformly to all businesses, foreign
and domestic. And the grounds for such claims appear to be expanding. For
example, a European mining company operating in South Africa is challenging
that country's black economic empowerment laws, seeking compensation from
the government for being required to recruit a certain number of blacks for
their workforce and board. Such cases can have a chilling effect on a developing
country's attempts to improve its social and environmental performance without
fear of being sued by foreign investors and having to pay them compensation
for the privilege of meeting its obligations to its own people.

In turn, the legal framework that regulates TNCs operates much as it
did long before the recent wave of globalization. A parent company and its

subsidiaries continue to be construed as distinct legal entities. Therefore, the parent company is generally not held liable for wrongs committed by a subsidiary, even where it is the sole shareholder, unless the subsidiary is under such close operational control by the parent that it can be seen as its mere agent. Furthermore, despite the transformative changes in the global economic landscape generated by far-flung networks of offshore sourcing, purchasing goods and services even from sole suppliers is still considered a transaction between unrelated parties. Factors such as these make it exceedingly difficult to hold an extended enterprise accountable for social and environmental harms inflicted by one of its units.

Of course, each legally distinct corporate entity is subject to the laws of the countries in which it is based and operates. But in most industries it has ready exit strategies. Moreover, states, particularly some developing countries, may lack the institutional capacity to enforce national laws and regulations against transnational firms doing business in their territory even when the government of the day has the necessary political will, or they may feel constrained from doing so by having to compete internationally for investment. In turn, the home states of TNCs may be reluctant to regulate against overseas harm by these firms because the permissible scope of national regulation with extraterritorial effect remains unclear in international law, or because the states' governments fear that those firms might lose investment opportunities abroad or relocate their headquarters.

Finally, this dynamic is not limited to TNCs. To attract investments and promote exports, capital-poor countries may exempt national firms from certain legal and regulatory requirements or fail to adopt such standards in the first place.

Recognizing the mounting challenge to their legitimacy, many of the world's leading TNCs have adopted their own private systems to manage various social aspects of their global operations, such as labor standards in their supply chains, or community engagement strategies in big-footprint natural-resource-extractive projects. Such voluntary initiatives are a positive development and help promote social standards. And they have important roles to play even in societies with well-functioning rule-of-law institutions and regulatory policies. But voluntary initiatives also have significant limits that need to be addressed and redressed. To state the obvious first, the vast majority of workers and communities live well beyond their orbit. However, even within their orbit, it is not unusual for workers in the same supplier factory, doing the same work, to be covered by different regulatory systems stipulated by different global buyers. This incongruity seems odd, to say the least, insofar as the rights in question are acknowledged to be universal.

These company-based systems are also highly variable. They may, but more often do not, meet internationally recognized standards even when those are explicitly invoked: in one case of what we might charitably term creative hermeneutics, freedom of association and collective bargaining were interpreted as "engaging in dialogue with employees about issues of mutual interest." Moreover, such voluntary systems vary in transparency, in what they reveal publicly about their inner workings and outcomes. Moreover, they vary in how proactive they are in anticipating and seeking to prevent problems, versus being reactive—typically, changing only when a company is confronted with some scandalous revelation in the press.

In addition, the driving forces that underlie the evident variability among corporate self-regulation include factors that have little to do with the substantive problems addressed, the specific populations involved, or the particular industry sector. In a recent survey of the Fortune Global 500 firms conducted by Ruggie, the specific rights recognized in a given company's corporate social responsibility (CSR) policy, and the external stakeholders that policy acknowledges, were found to be influenced decisively by the political culture of the company's home base, be it the United States, Europe, Japan, or emerging market countries.

At a more refined level of analysis, it is clear moreover that, among companies based in the same country and operating in the same industry, each firm's particular market segment strongly shapes the human-rights and broader CSR programs throughout its supply chains—the obvious comparison being between so-called premium brands, which trade on cachet, and value brands, whose consumers are concerned above all with price: the Nike–versus–Wal-Mart difference, in essence.

In sum, the existence of private corporate regulatory systems is surely a positive development. However, corporations' freedom to define both the form and the content of their regulatory systems and the high degree of market segmentation among such systems drastically limits their potential contribution to moving us toward an effective global business and human-rights regime, one that which would provide a sturdy social pillar to sustain the global market.

Multistakeholder initiatives and even collective business arrangements are typically clearer in the social standards they adopt and more transparent than private corporate regulatory systems. But in the end there is no substitute for governments doing what governments exist to do: to govern, and to govern in the public interest. Governments should not assume that they are helping business by failing to provide adequate guidance for, or regulation of, the adverse social impacts of corporate activities. On the contrary, the less governments do, the more they increase the risk to the reputation of the corporations that they should legitimately regulate. Governments need to promote a corporate culture respectful of human rights and environmental sustainability at home and abroad. And they need to consider the impact on such standards when they sign trade and investment agreements, and when they provide export credit or investment guarantees for overseas projects in contexts where the risk to those standards is known to be high.

Embedding the International Financial System

International capitalism has always, paradoxically, had an uneasy relationship to capital itself. The international financial architecture—the collection of norms and rules that structure the interactions between governments and international financial markets—has changed dramatically more than once. Capital has alternately been extraordinarily free and fundamentally constrained as international capitalism has evolved over time. No arrangement or orthodoxy has been permanent, although illusions of permanence, inevitability, and inexorability have defined each historical moment.

The first era of globalization, circa 1870 to 1914, was built upon fundamentally liberal institutional foundations embodied in the practices of the classical gold standard. Policymakers understood that to restrict freedom of capital violated the rules, albeit unwritten, of the gold standard. With restrictions considered to be neither normal nor legitimate, capital was as free to flow from one country to another as it has ever been. Bankers, managers, and investors thus enjoyed an age of extraordinary freedom and opportunity.

The effects of the First World War, the decade of recurrent international financial crises that followed, and the Great Depression destroyed that liberal order. Then, during the 1940s and 1950s, the rules of the international financial architecture were rewritten to be restrictive by design and according to an explicit doctrine. At that time members of the international financial community collectively shared a set of beliefs about the destabilizing consequences of short-term, speculative capital flows, or "hot money," and the need for government autonomy from international financial markets. Only a few decades earlier, these beliefs would have been considered radical and anticapitalist. At the time, however, capital regulation marked capitalism's way forward.

To regulate and control capital became the prevailing orthodoxy. Policymakers then wrote their new consensus into the international financial architecture. The right of members of the International Monetary Fund (IMF), European Community (EC), and Organization for Economic Cooperation and Development (OECD) to regulate movements of capital was protected by the IMF's Articles of Agreement (1945), the EC's Treaty of Rome (1957), and the OECD's Code of Liberalization of Capital Movements (1961).

As the rules were liberalized in the decades that followed, managers and investors enjoyed another era of freedom, one that spurred massive growth in global financial markets. Freedom of movement for capital became the new orthodoxy once again. Instead of the unwritten rules of the first era of globalization, this new era espoused formal, codified rules that explicitly defined its liberal principles and policy practices. The rules of the European Union (EU) and the OECD were rewritten to oblige members, the world's thirty or so richest countries, to allow virtually all cross-border flows of capital. The IMF began informally to promote capital liberalization among its membership, which was nearly universal, and some policymakers sought to amend the Articles of Agreement to oblige members to liberalize capital movements. Central bankers meeting in Basel at the Bank for International Settlements (BIS) endorsed this liberal evolution of government practices, allowing banks to measure their own risks using models of their own design. A shadow banking system emerged, largely unregulated, perhaps half as large as the formal banking system. And private credit rating agencies, such as Moody's and Standard & Poor's (S&P), propagated the practices of this shadow system, and rather than blowing the whistle on excessive risk, they helped to disguise it.

Now once again a new orthodoxy of capital mobility has been undermined, this time by a wave of financial crises that struck emerging markets in the 1990s and, ultimately, by the panic of 2008—which has wiped out perhaps $30 trillion in asset values, and necessitating nearly $1 trillion in global write-downs so far. The EU, OECD, and IMF have since begun a general rethinking within the international financial community of the risks and benefits of capital liberalization. This rethinking has received ever more focused attention.

The United States must rethink its approach as well. Today, capital regulation once again marks capitalism's way forward. Regulation should aim at two objectives that informed capital's place in embedded liberalism: greater insulation of the real economy from the effects of financial crises; and greater policy autonomy from the short-term preferences of financial market participants.

These objectives have never been pursued for their own sake, but to permit and promote free trade in goods and, later, services by buffering the adverse effects of such freedom. Financial crises and wildly fluctuating exchange rates caused by perhaps excessively mobile capital and boom-and-bust cycles have in fact historically undermined the kinds of cross-border transactions that almost everyone has always believed would contribute to world growth and employment: simple, comparatively prosaic trade. Domestic regulations and the international financial architecture should be organized to privilege current-account transactions (and particularly trade in goods and services) over financial-account transactions.

The compromise of embedded liberalism also privileges the judgment of policymakers over those of financial market participants. Governments, according to this way of thinking, should be relatively autonomous from market forces, free to pursue expansionary monetary and fiscal policies without endangering their exchange-rate commitments or suffering the outflow of capital in search of a higher rate of interest or a lower rate of inflation.

With regard to the international financial architecture, then, international organizations should not promote—nor should their charters legally oblige—capital liberalization. National governments should fulfill their responsibilities to their citizenries and commit themselves to freer trade in goods and services, but requiring full capital liberalization without also creating effective regulatory underpinnings can undermine their capacity to do so. Such regulatory underpinnings can help prevent implicitly guaranteed financial institutions from taking excessive risks; limit the public's exposure to the risks that are inevitably taken, partly as a consequence of the circumvention of rules that necessarily tends to follow market innovations; and restrict credit and asset bubbles as they are forming. International organizations and their rules have proven far more effective at encouraging liberalization than at cultivating domestic institution building. They should also promote regulatory practices that have proven to be most effective, and allow for constrained and temporary deviation from openness when domestic needs require such a choice.

True, this implies that we will trust policymakers more than the financial markets, and doing so is never easy. During the 1920s and 1930s, the West learned to mistrust unregulated financial markets. And then we forgot. Today, we are relearning that lesson. Although the next generation of policymakers will no doubt forget it again, the need to re-embed the financial markets is, momentarily, crystal clear. Failing to do so will undermine the legitimacy of the entire enterprise of global capitalism itself.

Domestic regulatory systems, including that in the United States, should privilege the real economy over financial sectors. This will require real public oversight, rather than, as the United States has done for so long, the outsourcing of regulatory authority to rating agencies. More broadly, excessive credit creation and flawed compensation schemes drew managerial talent into activities that, in retrospect, have destroyed billions of dollars worth of value. A re-embedding of the financial system would also thereby temper a variety of adverse consequences of credit bubbles, which misallocate both capital and talent. We should be prepared to live with trading some extra financial innovation for a smaller crisis next time.

Reviving Multilateralism

The compromise of embedded liberalism was, lastly, based on multilateralism. Among the many advantages of multilateral decision making is the legitimacy of the deliberative process. Power usually is far more effective when exercised with consent rather than coercion. Multilateralism is self-interest for the farsighted. The convenience of unilateralism is ephemeral and ultimately self-defeating because of the reactions that it inevitably provokes.

Recall the point of view of Thrasymachus, in the first book of Plato's *Republic*. In a classic Socratic dialogue, Thrasymachus and his colleagues debate the concept of justice. Impatiently, Thrasymachus seeks to ends the debate with a power-politics sort of definition: justice, he says, is merely the will of the stronger. The strong define right from wrong, and the weak must live with the result.

U.S. policy has been based too much, and for too long, on this notion of Thrasymachean justice. The momentary usefulness of unilateralism has been far outweighed by the growing number of countries whose policymakers now prefer to impede progress on important issues based on the principle of opposing—in effect, balancing against—the United States. The American approach to ad hoc globalization has been self-defeating. Instead, multilateralism and governance through international organizations need to be revived if this global economic order is to be saved. This can be accomplished in two ways.

First, the United States should pursue its interests through organizations like the IMF and UN, rather than embrace the expediency of unilateralism or the power asymmetries of bilateral deal making. Whenever possible, bilateral treaty negotiations should be abandoned in favor of multilateral solutions, which, though they require more compromises, are longer-lasting arrangements.

Second, the voting weights of several of the major international organizations must change in order to reflect the economic realities of the twenty-first century. The IMF is the place to start, for the organization's voting weights, established in 1944, no longer reflect a world in which the capital-rich Middle East and Asia must be part of any conversation about how to cultivate the multilateral cooperation that is so urgently needed. This means that individual European countries and the United States will have to see their voting weights shrink.

Why should the West voluntarily give up voting power in such organizations? The answer is simple. In the future, the United States could, for example, have 17 percent of the weighted votes in an irrelevant IMF, or 14 percent in an organization that actually matters—and 17 percent of zero is still zero. And irrelevance is inevitable in the absence of change, in part because systemically important countries ranging from Brazil to China to the United Arab Emirates have been forced into the role of only being able to spoil multilateral negotiations that do not include them, rather than contributing to discussions that reflect their needs and interests as well. Much the same is true of the UN Security Council, which now has two sets of permanent members: the P5, victors of World War II, with veto power; and a rotating bloc of "spoilers," whose driving motivation is to resist or undermine the decrepit hegemony of the P5 unless their immediate self-interest is advanced by it.

Cooperation will be essential in this next moment of the current era of globalization, and the United States is not in a position to demand or to force its emergence. It will have to emerge deliberately, legitimately, and multilaterally. The United States can maintain the ephemeral power of codified voting weights in dying organizations, or reinvigorate the organizations while taking roles better suited to the world in which we actually live.

Conclusions

"The world," Ernest Hemingway wrote, "is a fine place and worth the fighting for." His sentiment even holds true for the world economy, which has become in many ways more integrated than it ever has been. Globalization has helped to raise the living standards of millions; it has led to unprecedented opportunities for both societies and individuals. This integrated global economy is worth saving. The best way to save globalized markets is, perhaps paradoxically, to regulate them according to principles that, until very recently, have been very much out of fashion. Living in an era of neoliberalism, many of our policymakers lost track of the lessons of embedded liberalism. The result is paradoxical, for it was embedded liberalism itself that made possible the recent era of globalization through its embedded market practices—giving people the confidence that the risks of market opening would be shared. Social legitimacy—not neoliberal ideology—made the world safe for global markets. The influence of neoliberalism came late and was remarkably short-lived. The disembedding of markets and the asymmetrical rules governing TNCs have, more recently, undermined the very global project neoliberalism was meant to enhance.

Now this era of globalization must be saved, and not by the neoliberal ideology that led in significant part to globalization's current crisis of legitimacy. Rather, policymakers should return to the intellectual and normative framework that made the renaissance of global markets possible: embedded liberalism. The specific practices will need updating, but the core regulatory principle of this philosophy is essential: global markets require social legitimacy if they are to be sustained. That legitimacy derives from the embedding of market practices in the values and principles of national societies and, most broadly, in global civil society. In this essay, we have emphasized the relationship between social pillars and transnational business activity, the balance between the financial markets and the real economy, and the political advantages of multilateralism. Many other issues fit within this framework.

The United States has, for some years, violated the regulatory principles and policy practices of embedded liberalism, and the result has not been satisfactory. Global markets have been rendered illegitimate, though the country needs those very markets. Skepticism is on the rise, though the United States has benefitted greatly from this era of globalization. The failure of neoliberalism presents an extraordinary opportunity for policymakers to credibly overturn one regulatory model in favor of another; perhaps this choice would have been politically impossible just a few years ago. Today the principles of embedded liberalism are clearly essential, and we need them more than ever.

Acknowledgments

A book about "new perspectives" naturally relies on contributions from many quarters. As editors, we have many debts. First and foremost, we are deeply indebted to all of the chapter authors, who provided vital perspectives on regulation for a broad audience and on a remarkably tight time schedule. The book literally would not exist without them, and we are honored to have had the chance to work with them.

We are also profoundly grateful to the Tobin Project, its exceptional staff, and its friends and supporters. *New Perspectives on Regulation* is one piece of the Tobin Project's broader initiative on Government and Markets, which aims to increase understanding of the public role in facilitating a healthy economy and society. The Tobin Project staff has been indispensable to the completion of this book. Sage Trombulak organized the meeting of book contributors that began the writing process in earnest. Darin Christensen, Melanie Wachtell, and Jason Zahorchak all have done vital editorial and operational work that has improved the book's content and broadened its reach. Rebecca Chang's exceptional contributions to the editorial process have been enormously helpful. Mitch Weiss, the organization's Executive Director, supported this effort in every way and helped guide and discipline our thinking at many crucial points. We are grateful to all of these members of the Tobin team.

The Ford Foundation has played a central role in funding the Tobin Project's Government and Markets initiative, and we wish to thank Katherine McFate and Leonardo Burlamaqui at Ford for their valuable encouragement and advice.

Several of the contributors to this volume first met in 2008 at the Tobin Project's inaugural Government and Markets conference, entitled "Toward a New Theory of Regulation." That conference was made possible in part through the support of the Howard Gilman Foundation, which (along with Ford) provided funding and which hosted the conference at the beautiful White Oak Conference Center in Yulee, Florida.

We also wish to express our thanks to Jonathan Cedarbaum for helping us to think across chapters and for summarizing the work for policymakers; to Kristen Argenio for her outstanding design and layout work; and to Christopher Caines for his careful editing and suggestions.

One additional group that made this book possible is the policymakers who work with the Tobin Project on an ongoing basis, giving their time and energy to meet with scholars, attend conferences, and help identify the most pressing questions in need of attention. We remain enormously grateful for their important and continuing contributions.

James Tobin (1918–2002), the Nobel economist from whom the Tobin Project draws its inspiration and name, noted in *Essays in Economics* that, "the most important decisions a scholar makes are what problems to work on." Our deepest acknowledgement is to the spirit of public service that he left to all of us, and to the authors who, with their interest in constructive dialog and public questions, carry on Professor Tobin's legacy and stand as a sign of what American academia can be.

David Moss and John Cisternino, Editors

CPSIA information can be obtained at www.ICGtesting.com
Printed in the USA
LVOW10s0505090913

351528LV00002B/277/P